# THE
# CHAMPIONSHIPS
# WIMBLEDON

## Official Annual 1992

## JOHN PARSONS

*Photographs by*
BOB MARTIN, CHRIS COLE *and* GARY M. PRIOR

CHAPMANS

First published 1992 by Chapmans Publishers,
141–143 Drury Lane, Covent Garden, London WC2B 5TB

ISBN 1 85592 609 1

Designed by Philip Mann/ACE Ltd
Produced by Geoff Barlow

Typeset by Dorchester Typesetting Group Ltd, Dorchester
Origination by Studio One Origination Ltd
Printed in Great Britain by Butler & Tanner Ltd, Frome

This book produced with the assistance of Nikon (UK) Limited

# FOREWORD

It gives me great pleasure to write the foreword for the 1992 Annual.

Yet another Wimbledon is over, and Steffi Graf won her fourth final in grand style, while André Agassi became the new men's champion after a titanic struggle against Goran Ivanisevic. The Championships were considered to be one of the best – great weather for the first seven days, and great matches every day.

The fears that the game would be dominated by the big serve seemed groundless, as we had some outstanding men's matches. Yes, Sampras and Ivanisevic, among others, served quite a few aces – but, as always, the return of service was paramount.

This Annual captures the excitement of the wonderful tennis; also the enthusiasm of the fans, particularly on the middle Saturday when the 'Wimbledon wave' returned to both Centre Court and Court 1. Then, after the tension and thrill of the final weekend, there was the added bonus of the extra Monday. A full-house on Court 1 was there to salute the mixed doubles and gentlemen's doubles finalists. McEnroe and Stich fulfilled the desire and expectation of the crowd by winning 19–17 in the fifth set after five hours of tennis.

All this and more is recorded in the following pages. A wonderful and permanent record of the 1992 Championships. I wish the reader as much enjoyment as I had watching during the fortnight.

J.A.H. Curry
*Chairman of The All England Club and the Committee of Management of The Lawn Tennis Championships*
July 1992

# INTRODUCTION

Rarely has the Wimbledon fortnight been awaited with greater interest, curiosity and fascination than in 1992. And just as rarely have all the hopes and expectations been so wonderfully fulfilled.

The possibilities when the tournament began, in the brilliant sunshine that reflects those treasured 42 acres of London SW19 in such a colourful and evocative fashion, were endless.

Could, for instance, Monica Seles return to keep the engagement she had cancelled at the last minute a year earlier, and win the only one among the four Grand Slam tournament titles that was still eluding her? Or could Steffi Graf, having demonstrated at the French Open that her match-winning forehand was almost back to its best, fend off all challengers once again and retain the trophy with a fourth win in five years?

There were also, of course, others to consider – Gabriela Sabatini, the 1991 runner-up, who might easily have been returning as champion, had her serve not let her down; Jennifer Capriati, the youngest of the major contenders; and, at the other end of the age scale, Martina Navratilova, 35, living testimony to the belief that 'you're only as old as you feel' and still confident that she could add to her record nine wins.

If finding the winner for the ladies' singles seemed difficult, then predicting the outcome of the men's event was well-nigh impossible. Including Michael Stich, the defending champion, there were five champions in the draw, of whom three at least – Stich, Stefan Edberg and Boris Becker – could make out a persuasive case for winning it again.

As for the other two, John McEnroe and Pat Cash, the draw lined them up to meet in the second round. Here surely was the prospect of an early match capable of setting the whole tournament excitingly alight.

Without doubt, however, the most successful player on the men's tour arriving at Wimbledon was Jim Courier who, like Monica Seles, was holder of the Australian Open and French Open titles and was halfway to becoming the first player since Rod Laver in 1969 to win the men's Grand Slam. Although not always most comfortable on grass, he had after all been a quarter-finalist the year before, losing to Stich, who had described him as 'mentally the strongest right now of us all'.

And in a year dominated off-court by the apparent perils of power-serving, players such as Pete Sampras and, above all, Goran Ivanisevic – who had struck a tour record of 32 aces in one match against Edberg in Stuttgart – had to be considered.

Strangely enough, with hindsight, few people in the countdown to the 106th Wimbledon included André Agassi – who had dropped in rankings and seeding since his welcome return the year before – among their list of potential champions, except in passing . . . which is just what he proved he could do best when the action began.

As for Wimbledon itself, it too had undergone a major change since the year before, as more than 25 per cent of the spectators on Centre Court would appreciate. Immediately after the 1991 Championships, work had started to remove the old roof, with its 26 pillars, which had been bombed, patched and lifted since its original construction in 1922. In its place, the new roof, borne on just four pillars, provided almost everyone with a perfect view of the world's most famous and most beautiful court.

Despite the rain towards the end of the tournament, the attendances totalled 372,859, only 5,552 fewer than in 1991, which was artificially boosted by 24,000 on 'Middle Sunday'.

The pages that follow trace the many treats that were in store during a fortnight full of surprises, enterprising and exuberant matches and, even when it rained, some unexpected fun.

# 'YEEEEEESSSSS!'

DAVID ASHDOWN, PHOTOGRAPHER

André Agassi, shot by David Ashdown of The Independent on a Nikon, the official camera to The Championships Wimbledon.

# THE
# CHAMPIONSHIPS
# WIMBLEDON

# DAY

# 1

## Monday 22 June

On the opening day a year earlier only the caterers had been kept busy. It was so different for the launch of Wimbledon '92, when the weather stayed fine, most of the tennis was even better and 65 matches – thirteen more than during the whole of the first four days in 1991 – were completed.

This was also a day that began with a Royal Box thank-you to Dan Maskell, for his 41 years of broadcasting from Wimbledon. It continued in a similar sentimental vein, as Jimmy Connors made what many suspected would also be his last competitive appearance at The Championships.

The crowd's prolonged and affectionate appreciation for Dan, as a presentation was made to him by HRH The Duke of Kent, President of The All England Club, was naturally more sedate than the arrival and departure of the game's ultimate street-fighter, Connors.

When he walked out he slumped, like some elderly gent happy to have found a deckchair on the beach, into his seat at the side of the court. But it was a joke which, not too much later, was to hold a sad ring of truth. Against Luis Herrera, a Mexican left-hander not quite half his age,

the 39-year-old did his best to make the match fun, both for him and the packed, adoring crowd on Court 1, before in the end he had to submit 6–2, 1–6, 7–5, 6–3 to his more mobile opponent. The match was not easy for him but 'the show must go on'.

It was only the second time in 20 visits to Wimbledon that Connors, who had won the second of his two singles titles as much as ten years previously, had lost in the first round. But all the old defiance was there. Wielding his fluorescent yellow- and red- framed rackets with an exciting flourish, he recovered from a disastrous first set to play a second which was a joy.

From 2–4 down to 5–5 in the third, especially, the old swagger dominated the scene. Many of the shots played by both men were spectacularly athletic, as well as inventive, with Herrera demonstrating one marvellous piece of improvisation as he played a winning forehand – much to the chagrin of an opponent who probably felt he had the patent for such things – between his legs.

Yet the effort that Connors put into that third set took its toll. It ended with one of the most extraordinary points of the day. Connors, trailing 6–5, and having saved three

*Dan Maskell takes a final public bow at Wimbledon, alongside HRH The Duchess of Kent and John Curry, Chairman of The All England Club, during the presentation to mark his retirement, after 41 years as BBC Television's 'voice of Wimbledon'.*

*Stefan Edberg, as ever, reaching for the sky.*

*Previous page: 'It's easy when you know how,' Luis Herrera seems to be joking as he takes control against one of his heroes, Jimmy Connors.*

set points in his previous service game, found himself break point down again. Herrera played a net cord that looked like a winner, but Connors somehow dashed in to retrieve it, only to see the Mexican tap an easy over-head past him as the two players came almost close enough at the net to shake hands. One set later, that is precisely what they were doing.

At the end, when Herrera could hardly have responded more joyfully had he won the title, there was only a brief wave from Connors in response to the crowd's standing ovation. He was to drop more than a hint that he was beginning to think it was time for the old hero to ride off into the sunset.

After an even more exhausting experience at the French Open a month earlier, the American had talked of 'going beyond the wall and into a dark hole'. After this latest effort, in which he had offered one last epic piece

*The stress and strain on Jimmy Connors' face are unmistakeable. At 39, and making his 20th Wimbledon appearance, the former champion thrilled the crowd with one vintage set and glimpses of the old mischievous magic, before yielding to the ravages of time.*

of defiance by saving four match points, he said, 'Basically, playing three out of five sets isn't worth the pain any more. My hips go, my knees stiffen and my back gets sore. I hurt every day. I've dedicated so much of my life to tennis that it's time for me to do what I want to do.'

Connors, for so long the world number one, was of course unseeded, like another former champion, John McEnroe, who still had to start what became his memorable campaign. So the other 'golden oldie' on whom the spotlight fell, on the first day when all eleven seeds in action safely negotiated their first-round hurdles, was Ivan Lendl.

Playing his 13th Wimbledon only a matter of days before his American citizenship was confirmed, the 10th seed avenged his defeat at Queen's Club two weeks earlier by Patrick Kuhnen, a German ranked 97 – but only after once more experiencing some of those all-too-familiar problems on grass, which have prevented him from winning the only major title still missing from his fine record.

Lendl, who won 6–1, 7–6, 7–6, went some way towards acknowledging, like Connors, that the legs no longer respond agilely or consistently enough to instructions coming from the brain, when he said, 'I think I'm hitting the ball just as hard as I used to but maybe now with a little less confidence. I think, maybe, the point is that the game has improved, in that now everybody just goes for everything.'

The briefest glance, not only at the show courts but at all the others outside, especially where seeded players were fending off exuberant challenges from young or less experienced pretenders, would have shown that to be true. It was not just the number of aces to be seen, but the enormously powerful groundstrokes.

According to the bookmakers, Stefan Edberg, the 1988 and 1990 champion, was favourite to become champion again when the tournament started; but there was a salutary note of caution, applying both to himself and to Jim Courier, from the London-based Swede, after he had played what he called 'a reasonable match' to beat American qualifier, Steve Bryan – a sturdy right-hander making his Wimbledon début – 6–1, 6–3, 6–0. Things went well enough in the first set, which Edberg won in 25 minutes, but the double fault he delivered, to be broken when serving for the second set at 5–2, provided an ominous reminder of similar, much more ill-timed lapses in the past.

'I know that on a good day I can beat anybody, providing I stay focused,' he said. 'But I guess Courier feels the same now. He's very confident, but there's always going to come a day when you know things are not going that well. It's just a matter of time.'

*Alexander Volkov, the 15th seed, had a few hair-raising moments before overcoming a passive Emilio Sanchez (right) in four sets.*

*Jim Courier (left), the top seed, beginning the search for his grass-court dream.*

With hindsight, we can see that the prophecy of the man who, nearly four months before Michael Stich won Wimbledon in 1991, had picked Stich out as a possible contender (when no one else even had him on an extended short list) would come true again.

For the moment, though, all the established favourites, including Courier – the hard-hitting and even harder-working Australian and French champion, who was saying, 'I don't think it's wise for anyone to expect to be in the final, this early' – could be well pleased with their first day's work. Apart from Edberg and Courier, Boris Becker, Michael Stich, Pete Sampras and Goran Ivanisevic all advanced without creating too many ripples.

Becker, in particular, must have been encouraged by the speed with which his serve and volley game slipped back into place on the Centre Court against the Italian, Omar Camporese, who had twice the previous year stretched him to five sets with his own brand of aggressive tennis. The German, who had won the last of his three Wimbledon crowns in 1989, hit 12 aces but much

19

*Petr Korda concentrated well to beat Christian Bergstrom.*

*Amanda Grunfeld (right) from Lancashire upset the rankings with her fighting performance to beat Germany's Silke Meier (above).*

*Mark Petchey towels down on the way to beating American qualifier, Dave Randall, at 558 the lowest-ranked player in the 1992 Championships.*

*Early defeat for Sarah Loosemore during her break from studies at Oxford University.*

more heartening than that, for a player desperately short of match practice after injury, was his high percentage of first serves.

Just as 'Ladies' Day' on the first Tuesday now receives only token recognition, so matches in the ladies' singles have steadily encroached on the opening day of The Championships in recent years. This time even the top seed, Monica Seles, immediately entered the scene. Her 6–2, 6–2 defeat of Australian Jenny Byrne was routine enough on a day when some of the reporters from the tabloid newspapers arrived armed with gruntometers to measure the decibel level of the two-tone noise every time she hit the ball. It was a noise which had become just as much associated with her as those screaming double-handed passing shots.

There was too, almost inevitably, yet another inquest

into Miss Seles's late withdrawal from Wimbledon a year earlier. 'I never expected that me not playing Wimbledon would cause so much controversy,' she said, with patience and a tolerant smile, as she repeated the saga of the shin splints injury.

Finally, on the first Monday, Amanda Grunfeld, Mark Petchey and Chris Wilkinson all provided pleasure for British tennis with first-round victories that justified the wild cards they had been granted. Wilkinson was the happiest, and his performance probably the most impressive, as he beat Gianluca Pozzi from Italy, the world's 55th best player according to the rankings (which make no allowance for surfaces), 6–3, 6–3, 2–6, 7–6. 'It was the best feeling, my biggest win,' commented the Southampton player, who admitted that 'being on the next court to Mark [Petchey] and knowing he'd won, urged me on.'

# DAY 2

*Tuesday 23 June*

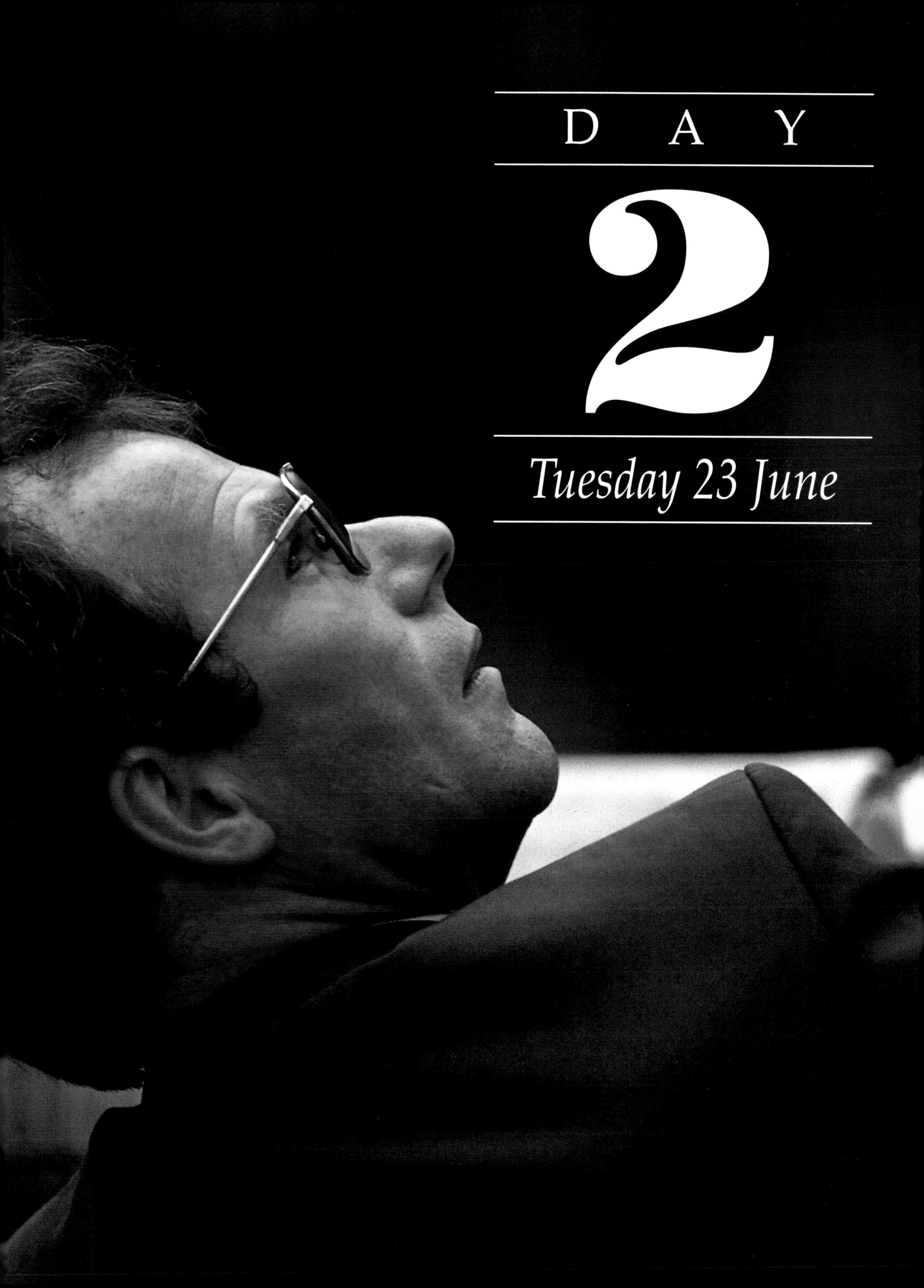

The delight over those British successes was, of course, mild compared with what followed a day later, when Jeremy Bates achieved an astonishing straight-sets victory over Michael Chang, the seventh seed, before an excusably partisan crowd on Court 14. British victories on this scale have not been commonplace anywhere in recent years, let alone at Wimbledon, where they make the greatest impact.

True, 12 months earlier Nick Brown, in his valedictory appearance as a singles player, had splendidly taken advantage of one of those days when Goran Ivanisevic was still, as he said, 'crazy in my head'. But in purely statistical terms, Bates's win was the best by a British player in the men's singles since John Lloyd had beaten fourth-seeded Roscoe Tanner, 15 years earlier.

'I've beaten top-ten players before, but this is definitely the best place to do it,' said the British number one from Solihull, after a 6–4, 6–3, 6–3 victory over an opponent who, three years earlier at the age of 17, had become the youngest winner of any Grand Slam tournament's men's singles title by capturing the French Open.

Bates broke the pitifully weak service of Chang no fewer than seven times, and although he dropped his own serve three times, he always looked comfortable after squeezing through a fluctuating first set. His one worry, after taking the second set more easily, came when he dropped his serve for what proved to be the last time at the start of the third set.

'Breaking back in the next game was vital,' Bates observed, recalling a brilliant backhand return down the line which did the task for him. 'There had definitely been a new spring in Chang's step at the start of that game, but it went down again after that. I think he got a bit depressed.'

The Bates triumph took 2 hours 18 minutes, and it was noticeable how the only spare seats there had been in the Press Box filled to overflowing, as news spread to those watching more fashionable names and reporters dashed from other parts of the ground to watch the final stages of the match. Bates did not fail them. He saved three break points to lead 4–1 in the final set and then held again under intense pressure to reach 5–3, when he served for the match.

Again he faced break points, one before his first match point, and another two points later, as he steadfastly refused to give ground against an opponent whose own terrier-like instincts had helped him escape from eight match points before losing in Paris. In the end Bates, 30, saved a third break point with a stunning backhand volley, forced a forehand error to reach match point for a second time, and took it with another crisp backhand which led to Chang limply netting a backhand.

*No matter how valiantly he huffed and puffed, Michael Chang could not blow away Jeremy Bates.*

*Previous page: A net-cord judge confirming his call to the umpire.*

*It was always an uphill battle for Britain's Andrew Castle (left) against Mexican, Leonardo Lavalle.*

*Pat Cash's assured volleying was vital against Holland's Jacco Eltingh.*

*A moment of reflection for John McEnroe, who lost the first set to Luiz Mattar.*

*Gigi Fernandez (right) with an eye on the ball – and aiming high.*

'This is only one win. I'm not playing it down, because it's one of the best I've had in twelve years, but it's not going to change the face of British tennis overnight,' said Bates, determined to try and keep things in perspective. 'I just wish there were more British players. I think all of us wish there was more competition and that fifteen or more British players went directly into the main draw on merit. If that was the case, then the whole environment would be better,' he added.

Absolutely right. But this outstanding start to what was to become an even more impressive period in Bates's career could not have been better timed, for it came just when many other indicators of progress in British tennis were falling encouragingly into place – though, sadly, not all.

The cheers for the Bates triumph had hardly died away when Jo Durie's 16th Wimbledon became one of her least distinguished as she lost, in truth none too surprisingly, 6–4, 6–2 to Linda Harvey-Wild, the American whose name was normally to be found only at the bottom of most tournament reports until she ousted Martina Navratilova at Eastbourne the previous week.

Andrew Castle, who could have been found almost as frequently in a television commentary box as on the tennis courts during the previous few months, never looked like reaching for the sky, as he surrendered in three sets against the Mexican left-hander, Leonardo Lavalle, 6–4, 6–0, 7–6. Castle lost ten consecutive games at one stage and then double-faulted at 4–4 in the tie-break, on a day when, Bates apart, the only British winner was Dorset's Shirli-Ann Siddall, who beat Plymouth's Valda Lake in three sets.

Meanwhile Pat Cash, playing only his fifth tour event (three of them in Britain) since he went into semi-retirement after his disappointing exit from The Championships the previous year, was lining up the tastiest of second-round clashes against John McEnroe, another former champion still not quite able to make up his mind about retirement.

'It'll be a thrill to be out there playing him again,' said the Australian, after a far from inspiring 6–4, 6–4, 7–6 defeat of Holland's Jacco Eltingh, as he let his mind roll back to their semi-final clash on Centre Court in 1984. 'A lot of things have happened since then,' he added, almost wistfully.

Eight years on, Cash, the Wimbledon champion in 1987, is at a stage in his career when he picks and chooses the few tournaments that most appeal to him, with

*Magdalena Maleeva (above) lost 6–2, 6–2 but was never afraid to take risks against Martina Navratilova.*

*Monique Javer's second-set recovery then faltered against the higher-ranked American, Marianne Werdel.*

Wimbledon at the top of the list. His ranking has slipped so low (191) that he had to rely on a wild card to be playing at all.

'It's going to be good. I'm quite going to enjoy it,' he said, as he looked ahead to what, a few years ago, would have been most people's idea of a dream final. As it was, there had not been too much evidence of Cash enjoying the match against Eltingh, when he was lucky that the Dutchman, fresh from winning in Manchester, was unable to maintain his challenge at the moments of greatest pressure. That was so not only when Eltingh was broken in the 10th game of both the first and second sets, but also in the closing stages of the third-set tie-break when, perhaps intimidated by a perfect Cash volley on the previous point, he tamely netted a backhand volley to trail 3–5.

Although there had been plenty of winning serves and volleys from Cash, somehow the old spark was missing. Apart from occasional flashes of inspiration, for many in the crowd the greatest thrill came at the end when Cash went through his familiar routine – with greater generosity than ever, it seemed – of distributing his own brand of millinery. Handfuls of headbands were scattered into the air, with another batch being handed to a

blushing ball girl, who made sure they were distributed only to those who had worked the match with her, while those arriving for the next match sought such souvenirs as well.

For his part, McEnroe recovered from a sluggish, out-of-touch start to beat Luiz Mattar of Brazil 5–7, 6–1, 6–3, 6–3. There was little hint of the magic that was to flow from his racket later in the tournament, both on his own and with Michael Stich in the doubles, so delaying his departure to the NBC Television commentary box in order to share his tennis talent with an even wider audience.

Early on, McEnroe's timing was erratic, but it all started to change from the fourth game of the second set when Mattar, who had been serving effectively, double-faulted to go break point down. McEnroe pounced with a classic forehand down the line, which seemed to jog his memory of how he used to play.

While Monica Seles's principal contribution to the day was her appearance at The Lawn Tennis Association's Short Tennis exhibition, where she hit with the youngsters and told them how she had started to play tennis 'when the racket was bigger than I was', defending champion Steffi Graf made short work of Noelle Van Lottum,

*Sarah Bentley (above), one of the British wild cards, had little chance against the greater groundstroke power of seventh-seeded Mary Joe Fernandez.*

*Elena Brioukhovets found the going just too tough against Pam Shriver.*

*Overleaf: Seeking inspiration was not quite enough for Valda Lake as she lost the all-British clash with Shirli-Ann Siddall.*

31

a Dutch-born French player, 6–1, 6–0.

Holding the first game to love with an ace, two forehand winners and a forehand volley in just 72 seconds, Miss Graf's whole game swiftly fell into place, although she did not win the unofficial race against the clock in which several of the leading ladies seemed to be engaged.

That first-round honour went to Gabriela Sabatini, the 1991 runner-up, who took only 46 minutes, one minute fewer than Steffi Graf, to beat Switzerland's Christelle Fauche, 6–1, 6–1. Martina Navratilova, who was given a standing ovation from fans displaying such placards as 'Martina, you're an artist' and 'Your tennis always music', took 53 minutes to strike most of the right notes against Magdalena Maleeva, while Jennifer Capriati overpowered a nervous Chanda Rubin, who was then free to concentrate on the junior event, in 56 minutes.

Miss Navratilova summed up her performance as 'nothing special, nothing great and nothing bad' as she registered a 6–2, 6–2 victory, minus any of those nerves that have sometimes been hovering and made her tentative in early rounds in the past. As the youngest of the Maleeva sisters actually played quite well, and was willing to take the initiative given the slightest opportunity, it was rewarding for both players, as well as for the crowd.

If Cash's match, in qualifying to play McEnroe, had been a somewhat stereotyped affair, there was no lack of spectacle and flair once André Agassi emerged, all in white again, except for the flaxen ponytail to be seen flowing through the back of his cap, to face Andrei Chesnokov from the Commonwealth of Independent States.

In a match of ferocious hitting from the baseline, which was to become a style more and more familiar as the fortnight progressed, Agassi dropped the first set 7–5, took the second 6–1 and then, at 0–40, was within a point of going 3–1 down in the third when, after 83 minutes, bad light and a hint of drizzle in the air forced them off court at 7.08 pm.

Some of the rallies had been breathtaking with, interestingly enough, Agassi making more mistakes from the back of the court than when he started to risk moving to the net. His utter frustration at finishing one spectacular point by ballooning his forehand over the baseline prompted by no means his only outburst – but the first that umpire Jeremy Shales, with prompting from Supervisor Ken Farrar, decided needed a code violation. Just as the match had not finished, neither had that episode.

DAY

# 3

*Wednesday 24 June*

Day Three was one of mixed feelings for André Agassi. There can hardly be a worse time for anyone serving than to have to resume a match that has been interrupted with the score at 0–40. Sure enough, the designer-clad hippy double-faulted to go 3–1 down. Even so, it was not long before his recovery was under way. Volleying with increasing relish and far greater effectiveness than many had expected, no doubt thanks to the doubles matched he had played with John McEnroe at the French Open, he took a further 72 minutes to complete his 5–7, 6–1, 7–5, 7–5 defeat of Chesnokov.

As on the night before, many of the rallies were played at a hectic, as well as powerful, pace, with Chesnokov contributing much to the high quality of the points. Yet still niggling away inside Agassi was the altercation involving Supervisor Ken Farrar the night before. He alleged that he was deliberately being picked upon, a charge that Mr Farrar roundly dismissed as not only untrue but bewildering. Agassi said he had already informed tournament Referee Alan Mills that he would appeal against any fine that might follow. The row rumbled on.

Otherwise, on a day when four more British players lost – and Stefan Edberg continued to suffer some extraordinary lapses on what appeared to be the easiest points, finally winning 7–6, 6–3, 7–6 against the South African, Gary Muller – the main story featured Goran Ivanisevic, whose tennis can be as zany as his desire for patriotic, as well as personal, success is zealous.

The Croatian served 34 aces, received a code violation for racket throwing, played one point entirely with his right hand instead of with his left, and survived a typical minor brainstorm during a wonderfully entertaining and fulfilled display, which embraced the Centre Court.

Mark Woodforde, the genial, freckle-faced Australian who, for much of the time, was the victim of Ivanisevic's target practice, took it all in good part. Indeed, it was he who prompted the right-handed point played by the two left-handers when, in mock surrender as the aces continued to fly past him, he turned his racket round as if ready to play with the handle rather than the head.

Never one to need much prompting, Ivanisevic entered into the spirit by delivering a right-handed serve, and an all right-handed rally developed before

*Mark Woodforde was on the receiving end of 34 aces from Goran Ivanisevic.*

*Stefan Edberg (far left) wavered only briefly during a workmanlike defeat of South African, Gary Muller.*

*Previous page: A line judge taking a bird's eye view.*

*Overleaf: Sabine Appelmans (left) was left wondering what to do next against Monica Seles.*
*The joy of victory for Claudia Porwik (right) over Shirli-Ann Siddall.*

Woodforde, who waited in vain for an apparently stunned umpire to call 'let', sent a volley into the net. The point stood.

'You may as well go out there and have a bit of fun if you're just going to be bombarded with serves like that,' Woodforde said afterwards. 'What could I do? You either laugh or cry, and in front of all those people I'd rather laugh. Maybe if you'd taken away the serves it would have been an interesting match. Mostly when I was facing a second serve, I had the upper hand, but how many second serves did I actually see?'

It should have finished in straight sets. Ivanisevic led 5–1 in the third set when, having thundered down a host of winning serves in addition to his aces, some of them at 129 mph, he was not only broken twice but found it was his turn to look bewildered when Woodforde, much to the crowd's fascinated delight, took the third set in a tie-break.

Yet it was a brief respite. Ivanisevic recovered his poise and, as Woodforde put it, continued to 'out-cannonball' his opponent as he moved towards that total of 34 aces, which represented the most hit in a match on Centre

*Pete Sampras (above) could hardly afford to relax for one moment against attacking Australian Todd Woodbridge (right), especially when the first three sets all went to tie-breaks.*

Court since records have been kept with such accuracy. As we now know, the total was soon to be surpassed, although not even the higher figure of 37 which Ivanisevic was to produce in the final is a Wimbledon record. That belongs to Britain's former Davis Cup player and now a member of the Committee of The All England Club, John Feaver, who hit 42 aces against former champion John Newcombe on an outside show court – but still lost.

'People ask me: how can a skinny kid like you serve so hard, and say, "Jesus, what are you eating?"' said Ivanisevic after his extravagant demonstration of aces. 'But I say, "I eat normal. You don't have to be like Schwarzenegger to serve thirty or forty aces. You have to be born with the talent."'

'If Goran serves like that he has a great chance of moving into the second week, but if he starts to miss it, then a lot of players have a chance to beat him,' said the Australian, with a forecast that was not too far wide of the mark.

Ivanisevic's form, in a match which David Irvine of the *Guardian* felt would have been better suited to Bisley, not only stimulated those who had shown such concern over the dominance of service power in the game, through the advances in racket technology, but was typical of displays from several of the favourites on the day.

*Above: Some lucky spectator went home with a prize souvenir – André Agassi's shirt.*

*Opposite: British pair Andrew Castle and Miles MacLagan pressed Holland's Paul Haarhuis and Mark Koevermans to three competitive sets.*

*Arantxa Sanchez Vicario at full stretch as she became the first of the leading ladies' seeds to fall against Julie Halard of France.*

Though some dropped sets, none looked to be in more than fleeting danger. That was true of Michael Stich, the defending champion, who – once he had recovered from a fractious opening set on Court 2 – took charge to beat Amos Mansdorf, without further threat to his serve. Pete Sampras advanced 7–6, 7–6, 6–7, 6–4 against Todd Woodbridge, with much generous help from the Australian, who led 4–2 in the first set, 4–1 in the second and had a point for 5–4 in the third.

Making a rare excursion, for him, to Court 14, Ivan Lendl beat Arne Thoms 7–5, 7–6, 1–6, 7–5, but not before the German – who had beaten Lendl in Milan on an indoor court earlier in the year – had impressed the crowd enough to earn the standing ovation they were offering in response to his cheerful wave at the end. But for several double faults at crucial moments, Thoms, who led 6–4 in the second-set tie-break, might have had even more to celebrate.

It was squeezing room only at lunchtime around Court 5 as Richard Krajicek, after a shaky start, proved too powerful too often for fellow Dutch player, Paul Haarhuis, in a 7–6, 6–3, 6–1 victory. Krajicek never looked back from the point at 5–5 in the tie-break when he fell, scrambled up again and reached set point with a perfect forehand volley. For the first time since 1984, therefore, only one of the 16 seeds (Michael Chang) failed to reach the second round, although there had already been quite a surprise in the second-round matches, with Sweden's Nicklas Kulti, who had enjoyed the first and quickest victory on Day One, going out almost as swiftly, 6–1, 6–2, 6–2, to a qualifier, fellow countryman Henrik Holm.

Hard though they fought, neither Mark Petchey nor Chris Wilkinson could quite benefit from the inspiration of the Bates victory, for while both played reasonably well, both had the sort of chances which, at this level of the game, must not be missed. And they were.

Petchey, for instance, having pluckily clung on in the first set, saving four break points spread over three different games against Marc Rosset, was unable to sustain a 5–2 lead in the opening-set tie-break. He double-faulted away the initiative and was beaten 7–5, 6–2, 6–3. Then Wilkinson, who had not only won the first set on Court 3 (again alongside Petchey), but had continued to hold his vastly improved serve quite comfortably, was suddenly broken from 40–0 at 3–4 in the second. Not only that, but he held four set points and saved three before losing the crucial third set in what became a 3–6, 6–4, 7–6, 6–4 defeat by Sandon Stolle, son of former Wimbledon runner-up, Fred Stolle. The tension on both players in the 15–13 third-set tie-break was enormous. First serves, which at that stage could have produced a handsome dividend, were at a premium.

*Chris Wilkinson kept a packed Court 3 crowd on tenterhooks as he went close to beating Sandon Stolle.*

Similarly, two other British players, Amanda Grunfeld and Shirli-Ann Siddall, both lost matches they might have won. Miss Grunfeld, despite grittily pulling back from 1–5 in the final set, ultimately lost 5–7, 6–2, 7–5 to Japan's Mana Endo, a student teacher who had won the World Student Games title in Sheffield in 1991. Meanwhile Miss Siddall lost her way after a bright start against Germany's Claudia Porwik and was beaten 6–4, 6–2.

Not for the first time, all the seeds in the ladies' singles had come through the first round unscathed, but there was an early and unexpected victim in round two when Arantxa Sanchez Vicario, perhaps due to concentrating on the forthcoming Olympic Games in her home town of Barcelona, was surprisingly beaten 6–3, 2–6, 6–3 by the French girl, Julie Halard. Miss Sanchez was dominated by the former finalist in the girls' event, who had climbed to number 23 in the world rankings, as Miss Halard employed her powerful forehand successfully, to expose the Spaniard's limitations and uncertainties on grass.

Although she had lost at both their previous meetings, Miss Halard showed tremendous determination, saving six break points in one exhausting first-set game of eight deuces. But Miss Sanchez still believes that one day she will emulate Manuel Santana by winning Wimbledon for Spain. 'Maybe two years ago I thought I could not win on this surface but now my mentality has changed,' she commented. 'You always have to think positive, and when I improve a couple of things, such as my serve and my ability to win the important break points, then that will be the day when I can win Wimbledon.'

Monica Seles arrived at Wimbledon secretly, if not yet openly, convinced that her day was near, and the gulf in class was all too plain to see as she beat Belgium's Sabine Appelmans 6–3, 6–2 and then apologized for turning up the grunting level in the second set. She was, she insisted, very conscious of the need to eliminate a habit which even those who had excused it when she was a junior were now finding increasingly irritating.

A second seed departed from the ladies' singles. Kimoko Date, the 15th in the list of ranked favourites, was beaten 6–1, 6–3 by Gigi Fernandez, although on grass that was hardly a major upset. There was, however, just the hint of one developing late in the evening on Court 1, when Californian Kimberley Po fought back from losing the first set to take the second 6–3 from Martina Navratilova in fading light at 8.45 pm.

Any one of half a dozen matches deserved the billing 'Match of the Day' on the first Thursday, when Jeremy Bates marched on majestically; John McEnroe beat Pat Cash in a five-set thriller full of all that is best in the grass-court game; Boris Becker needed 20 aces and took nearly three and a half hours to stay in the tournament against a Czechoslovakian ranked 116; and Jennifer Capriati overpowered her American president (in the tennis sense, of course).

Domestically, it was another splendidly professional and polished performance from Bates, who kept the British flag flying into the third round, earning the biggest headlines and greatest prominence on the television news. After a gripping and crucial first set, when the tension on Court 1 extended to the spectators who were filling it, Bates edged through the tie-break and went on to beat Spain's Javier Sanchez with an impressive 7–6, 6–3, 6–4 win.

The crowd, almost afraid in the early stages to demonstrate their emotional support for the British number one – lest their developing expectations might be premature – emitted hardly a sound when he reached set point in that tie-break, on a Sanchez backhand error. From then on, however (like the man they were willing to win), they relaxed and were full of enthusiasm until, when Bates served out for victory, they responded with an enormous ovation.

For a second time Bates had reached the third round without losing a set, and he did so under the pressure of knowing that after eliminating Michael Chang, anything less than victory would have been regarded as a disaster, irrespective of how the match was played. 'Against Michael, I had nothing to lose. This was a match I really had to win, so to some extent it was an even better victory for me,' he said.

Total concentration, something which has not always been at the top of the list of Bates's qualities, was again the key, especially during the first set, which lasted almost an hour. Having failed to capitalize upon three break points in the fifth game, for instance, he then saved three from 0–40 in the sixth.

Wearing a protective sleeve to ease the strain on a right arm sore from extensive serving – he had been on court winning a first-round doubles match until 9 pm the night before – Bates then missed three more break points in the ninth game. That meant that instead of serving to take the opening set, he had to serve to stay in it. If he was going to crack, this was when it might have happened; but after starting the game with a low backhand volley into the net, a brilliant stop volley ended the doubts.

Although he double-faulted twice in reaching 6–6, and was still too tight to produce enough first serves, Bates

*The moment of triumph for Jeremy Bates on Court 1 against Javier Sanchez.*

*Overleaf: John McEnroe takes a break after one of many great points in his classic match with fellow former champion, Pat Cash, who still regularly re-tapes his racket handle.*

lifted his and everyone else's spirits (bar the Sanchez contingent) by spectacularly wrong-footing the Spaniard to reach 5–3 in the tie-break. Bates won his first set point with a penetrating backhand volley, which to some – but by no means all – looked wide.

'That first set was huge,' commented Bates. 'I noticed at the start of the second set that Javier eased off a little bit and his serve was easier to hit. I knew then I had a chance to take the initiative.'

Later, in the twilight of a memorable day and an even more memorable career, McEnroe punched the air with both fists to mark his unlikely victory over fellow former champion, Pat Cash, after 4 hours 38 minutes of always compelling tennis on the Centre Court. McEnroe, 33, had twice found the energy, will power and inspiration to recover from being a set down and beat the Australian 6–7, 6–4, 6–7, 6–3, 6–2.

To those of us fortunate enough to have witnessed these two former champions in their heyday, it was as if the clock had been turned back to a more subtle and skil-

ful age. Although early on there were moments when the lack of pace and penetration in too many shots betrayed their ages and recent lack of match play, these were more than compensated for by the nostalgic examples of competitiveness and natural, instinctive talent.

If the capacity crowd was not admiring the still-wondrous backhand volley control and power from Cash, then it was probably the brilliant touch-play of McEnroe near the net that was earning gasps of delight. All the old familiar signs were there, right down to the last twitch.

Anguish, relief, joy and despair, exhilaration and disgust – every emotion was bared, with McEnroe's greater hunger for success being decisive in the end.

The way he rallied from losing the tie-break 7–1 at the end of the 68-minute third set, and then four times in the course of three games saved break points in the fourth, was not only crucial but phenomenal. There was a standing ovation for McEnroe when he made it two sets all with an ace, but in his opening service game of the fifth set he had to save four more break points. But there was

*Eduardo Masso surprised André Agassi by taking the first set.*

no way now that he was going to bow out to a rival he had beaten on his way to the 1984 title, and whom he had described as 'still one of the best ten grass-court players in the world'.

McEnroe was now smartly jumping on to Cash's serves, particularly any that fell short, producing a sustained series of magnificent returns to take the last five games in amazing fashion. The ecstatic crowd stayed on their feet for three minutes, hailing a match that had transcended all that had gone before – and nearly, though not quite, all that was to follow before the main titles were won.

On this mainly sunny but heavily humid day, Jim Courier hardly had to sweat as he overcame Byron Black, a qualifier from Zimbabwe, 6–4, 6–1, 6–4. But winning so easily is not always an advantage, as the American was to discover so sensationally 48 hours later.

The ease and speed of Courier's progress meant that André Agassi followed him on to Court 2 rather earlier than he had probably expected, which may explain why he dropped the first set to the Belgian, Eduardo Masso, a left-hander who had won his first match on grass earlier in the week.

Agassi promptly tucked his flowing locks back under his cap for a 4–6, 6–1, 6–3, 6–3 victory, but he was still clearly fretting over the £850 fine that had been imposed for the words he had uttered out of place during the previous round. Admitting that he had sworn, but contesting the actual words supposed to have been said, and continuing with his allegation of a vendetta against him, Agassi remarked, 'I'm definitely going to appeal. It's not the money, it's the principle.' He was equally adamant that the incident would not harm the happy relationship that he now has with Wimbledon. 'I've learned to love the place and now realize it was a mistake for me to stay away in previous years.'

Becker, meanwhile, had to fight for his life in the gathering gloom on Court 1 before overcoming Martin Damm, a Czechoslovakian making his first appearance in the main draw. Damm, who had lost to Britain's Jonathan Haycock when top-seeded in the junior event two years before, served and volleyed with an uninhibited joy which even Becker, in the midst of crisis, must have admired and possibly envied.

Although the three-times former champion eventually escaped 4–6, 6–4, 6–4, 3–6, 6–3, it was only when he produced two aces on the last three points that he exorcised the apparent desperate vulnerability that had marked his performance. 'At 2–2 in the fifth, you start to get worried,' said Becker, trying to console himself that fighting his way out of such a severe test was 'just what I needed'. But deep down the German, who had sacked

*Boris Becker had a fight against Czechoslovakian Martin Damm (opposite, below).*

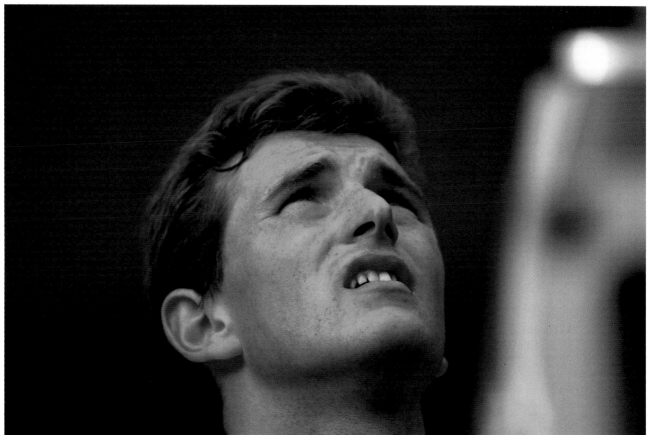

his coach Tomas Smid a week before The Championships following a disagreement over his Wimbledon preparation, knew that he was still way below his best, mentally and physically. How much longer, even other players were now asking, could he stay on the tightrope?

While Becker lived to fight again, Petr Korda, another Czechoslovakian, whose achievement in reaching the final of the French Open had carried him to sixth in the world rankings, was becoming the day's major casualty. On the anniversary of Wimbledon's longest match, between Pancho Gonzales and Charlie Pasarell, Jakob Hlasek recovered from two sets down to win 4–6, 3–6, 6–3, 7–6, 16–14.

Korda missed a match point in the fourth-set tie-break, but although the length of the match ultimately produced an exciting finish – with 44 consecutive games won on serve before the final, decisive break – it was more a test of endurance than enterprise.

Almost inevitably in the first week, the ladies were being overshadowed by the glut of compelling men's matches, but there was a good deal of interest as Jennifer Capriati, 16, hit 48 winners compared with only a dozen that she allowed Pam Shriver, president of the Women's Tennis Association, to deliver in this, her 14th year on the circuit.

Miss Shriver, a few days short of her 30th birthday on American Independence Day, could not live with Miss Capriati's greater groundstroke power; and it was much the same for the American, Marianne Werdel, as she managed only two games against Steffi Graf, who was beginning to look in ruthless form – especially with that forehand.

Gabriela Sabatini, moved from Centre Court to Court 2 because Cash and McEnroe had been taking so long, seemed unperturbed as she overwhelmed Isabelle Demongeot of France, 6–2, 6–3. Meanwhile, also in keeping with expectations, Natalia Zvereva upset the eighth seed, Conchita Martinez, whose antipathy to grass courts makes her a rare visitor, 6–3, 5–7, 6–4.

As for Martina Navratilova's unfinished match from the night before, whatever uncertainty there may have been in her mind then, when she was clearly pleased to stop at one set all, vanished when she stepped back on to Court 2 in bright sunshine. She swept through the deciding set without losing a game. With so much other excitement around, perhaps it was just as well.

# 5

It is not unusual for diversionary debates to achieve prominence at Wimbledon on matters great and small. Wimbledon '92 was no exception. Apart from that grunt which, much to the growing dismay and discomfort of Monica Seles, seemed to be most persistent, there were two other debates in the first week that enjoyed exaggerated attention.

For instance, was André Agassi wearing his white baseball cap all the time – on, and off, court – so that people would not notice that he was going bald? Eventually someone plucked up the courage to ask him. 'Are these questions for real?' he replied. End of debate.

It was on Day Five, however, that passions were really aroused, with a session which, depending on how seriously you took it all, could have come straight from a late-night discussion on Channel 4 or from BBC's Comedy Playhouse.

Holland's Richard Krajicek was to blame. Earlier in the tournament he had been quizzed by Dutch radio on the sensitive issue of equal prize money for men and women in tennis. Striking out as boldly as he does most of the time on his serve, he had embellished his opposition to the idea by casually suggesting that 'Eighty per cent of the top hundred women players are fat, lazy pigs.'

That did it. The moment that comment became known in the ladies' dressing room, they were after the 'Rotter from Rotterdam' (as they called him) just as vigorously as the 'Rotters from Fleet Street' (as tennis writers affectionately call their news colleagues), who were sharpening their pencils with glee.

Krajicek – who was hardly feeling too fit himself after just losing 4–6, 7–6, 3–6, 7–6, 6–2 to Frenchman Arnaud Boetsch – arrived in the interview room just moments after Martina Navratilova had left hissing ominously, 'My body fat is lower than his . . .' and adding, 'I'm going to go and beat him up.' Perhaps it was as well that by the time she slipped back into the rear of the interview room, ready to take issue with him, Krajicek was just leaving.

'People are forgetting that I said that the top women, such as Graf, Seles and those, deserve to have equal prize money, because they are good and people come to watch them,' Krajicek said, as if trying to douse the flames of fury. But he knew the damage had been done. On the basis that he might as well be hung for a pound as a penny, that is probably why he went on to admit that he had been exaggerating when he talked of 80 per cent of the girls being unfit. 'What I meant to say,' he continued, with an unmistakeable smirk on his face, 'was that only seventy-five per cent of them are fat pigs.'

Woe betide him if he ever decides to play mixed doubles.

As it happened, this lovely storm in a teacup coincided

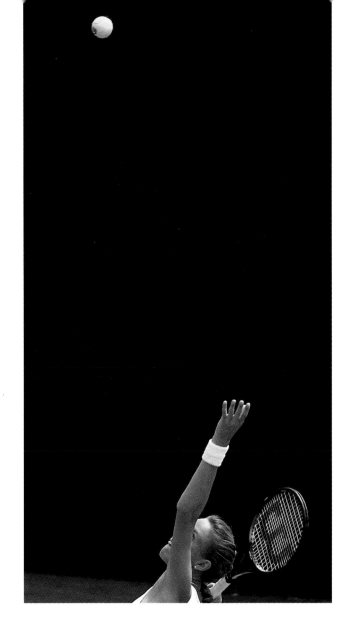

*Although she won the first set, victory remained out of reach for Australia's Nicole Provis (above) against fleet-footed Nathalie Tauziat.*

*Mary Joe Fernandez needed treatment after a heavy fall during her 6–3, 6–3 third-round defeat by fellow American, Amy Frazier.*

*The sun certainly shone on Mark Keil as he and Noelle Van Lottum beat veterans Paul Annacone and Elise Burgin in round one of the mixed doubles.*

with one moment of brilliant athleticism by Martina Navratilova. Of the many instinctive winners that the nine-times champion has hit at Wimbledon over 20 years, few have been more spectacular, as well as more significant, than the behind-the-back shot that stunned everyone, including herself and her young German opponent, Barbara Rittner, on Court 1. Miss Rittner, the 1991 junior champion, who had rallied from 2–5, had a point that would have offered her the chance to serve for the first set. Having set herself up with a brilliant lob, which sent Miss Navratilova scuttling back early in the rally, Miss Rittner let fly from within two yards of the net with a full-blooded double-handed backhand which, at any other time, would have been a winner. Yet somehow Miss Navratilova, also almost on top of the net by then, sprang round and played an amazing winner from behind her back.

'I've hit shots like that before, but I don't think I've ever done so at a better time,' said the fourth seed, who admitted that she felt she had been 'on the skids' after cruising at 5–3, 30–0. Miss Navratilova won the next two points to hold for 6–5, and the obvious swagger as she changed ends signalled that she felt the crisis had passed. She went on to win 7–5, 6–1.

Her victory took her through to meet Indonesia's

*Amy Frazier took full advantage of the injury to Mary Joe Fernandez for an impressive third-round defeat of her fellow American.*

Yayuk Basuki, another player who, by no stretch of the imagination, fitted the majority description given by Krajicek. She had upset 10th-seeded Anke Huber 6–2, 6–3, on a day when double faults by the German, who had been playing golf at Wentworth for relaxation between her matches, were as costly as double bogies.

Monica Seles, meanwhile, took time to establish her customary supremacy against Laura Gildemeister, but then looked increasingly at home on grass as she moved to a 6–4, 6–1 victory in 64 minutes, while Julie Halard followed up her defeat of Arantxa Sanchez Vicario by toppling Helena Sukova, 4–6, 6–1, 6–3.

The most prominent departure from the ladies' singles, however, involved Mary Joe Fernandez. The previous year's semi-finalist limped off Centre Court after falling heavily, damaging her thigh and arm, when her match with fellow American Amy Frazier was nicely balanced at 3–3 in the first set. And although Miss Fernandez continued after three minutes' injury time-out, she never recovered from losing five consecutive games. Miss Frazier won 6–3, 6–3.

In the men's singles, qualifier Henrik Holm continued to enjoy himself, upsetting 15th-seeded Alexander Volkov, a giant-killer himself in earlier Grand Slam tournaments, in four sets. Meanwhile Wally Masur, the Southampton-born Australian, reached the fourth round for the first time since beating John McEnroe in 1988, by outlasting the 13th seed, Brad Gilbert, in five sets.

Such performances, however, were the supporting acts on a bill that featured the impressive demolition of Scott Davis by Pete Sampras, 6–1, 6–0, 6–2, and the Court 14 shoot-out between two of the biggest servers in the game, Goran Ivanisevic and Marc Rosset.

Ivanisevic, who admitted that he had been apprehensive beforehand, need not have worried. He won the match 7–6, 6–4, 6–4 (and the ace contest 22–15), as the Swiss player missed too many first serves and threw in too many double faults – ten of them.

'Now I'd like to hit forty aces against Ivan Lendl, in the hope of beating him for the first time,' said the Croat. For his part, Lendl was happy simply to have produced a storming finish on Court 1 to escape in the fifth set against the unseeded Australian, Sandon Stolle.

It was a close thing. With Stolle, 21 – son of Fred, the 1963–5 singles runner-up – serving at 4–4 in the final set, Lendl, whose serving had been almost crazily erratic, offered feeble responses on the first two points. A second successive third-round exit was beginning to look imminent. Yet suddenly, as if remembering his promise when losing to Patrick Kuhnen at Queen's Club that if he was to be beaten at Wimbledon it would be with 'all guns blazing', Lendl produced one stunning forehand return down

*Australian Renee Stubbs in action in the doubles.*

*Ivan Lendl thrilled his supporters on Court 1 with many blistering winners in a last-gasp recovery which left Sandon Stolle (overleaf) down and out.*

the line, followed by an equally glorious backhand.

Stolle held for 5–4 but Lendl's mood had been transformed. Much to the delight of the unashamedly partisan crowd, which had already enjoyed plenty of success for other 'old friends' during the tournament, huge serves rained down as Lendl made it 5–5. Then, in the 11th game, Stolle was rocked by three of Lendl's finest returns of the 2-hour 30-minute match, earning a break for the former world champion, who then confidently served his way into the fourth round.

'There's no pressure on me at all because no one expects me to win any more,' said Lendl after his 6–3, 1–6, 2–6, 6–3, 7–5 progress. 'I lost my timing on the serve at the start of the second set and just couldn't recover it, but it began to come back in the fourth, and when I served well I was in control,' he added.

Stefan Edberg had no such problems. He took just 94 minutes to dismiss the South African, Grant Stafford, for whom everything had anyway been a bonus, after he was beaten in the last round of the qualifying and then was given his chance when a late vacancy occurred in the first-round draw. It was straightforward also for defending champion Michael Stich, with an air of inevitability about the outcome once the German had taken the first set from Magnus Larsson, a Swedish player with free-flowing strokes that sometimes flow too freely for his own good.

*Victory again for Michael Stich – but what would the future hold?*

Larsson had beaten Stich in Munich two months earlier but, as the third seed pointed out, 'That has no relevance to what happens here. I'm playing better tennis than last year,' Stich continued, after his 6–4, 6–1, 6–3 victory. 'It's not as risky, and it's a nice feeling to be through to the second week. For a start, there are fewer players in the locker room.'

Stich then returned to Centre Court with McEnroe for their second round of the doubles – though not for as long as they would have liked. At 8.12 pm, with the light fast fading, Referee Alan Mills walked on to court just after the defending and former singles champions had taken a two-set lead over John Fitzgerald and Anders Jarryd, 6–3, 7–6, in a 7–3 tie-break. Play was halted. The defending doubles champions were clearly relieved to be given what was to become more than just a one-night stay of execution, even though they lost in the end. McEnroe meanwhile made it abundantly clear to everyone that he and Stich wanted to play on.

*Drama as Jeremy Bates falls headlong, just two points from victory, against Frenchman Thierry Champion (right).*

While it may not quite have matched 'Middle Sunday' – which, however much officials would have liked to repeat it, would simply not have been practical – 'People's Saturday', when the first 2,000 in the overnight queue were able to snap up reduced-price Centre Court seats, was not only a great success but became a marathon one as well.

Having been greeted by a jazz band playing on Centre Court for the first time, the fans then sat back to wallow joyously, and sometimes in disbelief, as one of the greatest day's play in Wimbledon history unfolded. By the time what was probably the longest day's play in Centre Court history had ended – well over eight hours after it had started at noon – they had seen not only the top-seeded Jim Courier knocked out by a 193-ranked qualifier of whom most had probably never heard, but also swift virtuoso performances from Gabriela Sabatini and André Agassi before a tremendous tussle for Steffi Graf to complete the proceedings.

Not only that, but the regular, ever-louder cheers wafting over from Court 1 told them that the Jeremy Bates bandwaggon was still rolling. And if they had ventured

*Previous page: Steffi Graf had a tense struggle with South Africa's big-serving Mariaan de Swardt.*

*Boris Becker's experience proved vital against Bryan Shelton.*

*'That's life!' said a beaming Andrei Olhovskiy when asked how he had knocked out top seed, Jim Courier.*

further than the tea lawns when taking a breather from Centre Court, spectators might have enjoyed glimpses of a feast of doubles matches in full swing.

In reality the way in which Courier's Wimbledon and Grand Slam hopes were spectacularly crushed over 2 hours and 39 minutes by Russian qualifier, Andrei Olhovskiy, made the greatest impact – not least on the top half of the draw. But it was Bates's courageous triumph in becoming the first British player to reach the fourth round since Buster Mottram 10 years earlier that created unbridled domestic joy.

'I'm shattered beyond words at the moment,' said Bates as he savoured a 7–5, 6–4, 6–7, 4–6, 6–4 victory over the much higher-ranked Frenchman, Thierry Champion, who a year earlier had beaten both Pat Cash and then Nick Brown after the British player had despatched Goran Ivanisevic.

So often in the last two sets it seemed as if victory was slipping away from Bates. He lost a 3–0 lead in the third set and then the tie-break, which he started with a double fault. Often torn between the obvious need to attack at every opportunity and the risk of being passed or lobbed, Bates then had to save two break points in the second game of the final set, and three more two games later, before setting the Union Jacks waving once again with a flurry of great returns and wonderful serving in a

*Betsy Nagelsen (above), still as determined as ever in the doubles, in her 19th year on the circuit, as she and Ros Fairbank-Nideffer took former champions, Martina Navratilova and Pam Shriver, to three sets.*

*Ball girls tidy up after a match.*

rousing finish to the match.

At 2–1 in the final set, a ball boy handed the British player a note. Was it coaching? No, it was just a reminder from his physiotherapist to change his soaked shirt and sweater, because he looked to be dehydrating.

'Something was keeping me standing up, but I'm not sure what. I just lived on the belief that I could win. And to win like that at Wimbledon is really beyond words. 'I might not appear elated, but that's simply because I'm knackered,' he added, wearily but triumphantly, before going off to partner Jo Durie to victory in the first round of the mixed doubles.

Serving for the match, Bates's serve, which had faltered for a while in the middle of the match when he was frequently passed or lobbed, was suddenly revitalized. There were two service winners and then an ace before the perfect backhand winning volley, after almost four hours.

An explosion of cheering greeted the Bates win, not only within Court 1, but also outside, from those watching the scoreboard above The All England Club main entrance – and even on Centre Court, where André

Agassi was about to serve. He realized what had happened, walked away for a moment, waiting for the noise to stop, and then double-faulted, but it was only a minor disruption in his 6–3, 7–6, 7–5 defeat of fellow American, Derrick Rostagno.

The predictable nature of Agassi's success was probably a relief to the Centre Court crowd, still stunned from what had gone before, as Courier – so used to seeing his groundstrokes ramming opponents into submission – found his juggernaut skilfully derailed by a 26-year-old Muscovite, who had won only two other tour matches before arriving at The Championships as a qualifier.

Olhovskiy, who in all four of his Wimbledon visits had been forced, by his lowly ranking, to start in the qualifying competition at Roehampton, never allowed himself for one moment to be intimidated by the record and reputation of an opponent holding the Australian Open and French Open titles. Throughout his historic victory, Olhovskiy's serving and volleying, learned from playing on the old wood and plastic courts that used to be commonplace in Europe, were consistently brilliant. He took every opportunity to attack, while at the same time shrewdly varying the pace, to deny Courier the chance to find his groundstroke rhythm.

At the time, Peter Doohan's second-round defeat of Boris Becker in 1987 seemed unbelievable – the German was defending a two-year hold on the title. But this was the first time that a top seed had lost to a qualifier, and there was a delightfully refreshing, almost casual manner in which Olhovskiy (who is also a chess fan and has played tennis with Gary Kasparov) saved break points with aces, every time one felt that the world number one was about to restore some sense of order to the proceedings.

'I just play, I don't think about winning or losing,' said Olhovskiy, who had shrugged off the fatigue of a five-set doubles match the night before to produce the performance of his life. Courier, who had dropped only three sets in his previous 25 matches, took his defeat like a champion, saying of his opponent, 'He rose to the occasion and I was outplayed. He played well on the big points. That was the difference.' Meanwhile Olhovskiy, with plenty to tell his young son when he is old enough to understand, was asked if he could really believe he had beaten the world number one. He smiled and said, 'Life is life, you know. The difference between the top guys and the guys around two hundred is all in the head. If you have confidence you can play very well.'

He might have added that in addition to the difference being in the head, it is also in the pocket, although at that moment it did not seem to matter. As he pointed out, until a year beforehand he had been playing for the Sports Committee in Russia. Now this refugee from Communism, who (like Andrei Chesnokov) has the word *perestroika* engraved on his watch to remind him never to take personal freedoms for granted, keeps his prize money.

Olhovskiy, who had also reached the fourth round in 1988, was not alone among the qualifiers through to the last 16. Christian Saceanu, originally Romanian but now holding German citizenship, outlasted Jakob Hlasek over five sets and then faced the prospect of playing Agassi. Even on a day when his presence and performance had been overshadowed, the American's adrenalin was flowing with inspiration. 'I'm excited about still being alive. The vibes are so intense on Centre Court you can't help but be scared, nervous, intimidated all at the same time,' Agassi said, even though, as he was to prove with increasing authority during the second week, none of those dangers greatly worried him.

Next in line for Olhovskiy would be John McEnroe, who had looked in stunning form on Court 1, where he gave a quality grass-court lesson to David Wheaton, as he beat the 1991 semi-finalist 6–3, 6–4, 6–4 in just under three hours of sustained brilliance. He wavered but briefly, losing the first three games of the second set and immediately putting things right by winning the next five. His touch around the net was once more worthy of the greatest appreciation.

McEnroe did not need others to tell him that Courier's defeat had offered him the enticing prospect of reaching at least the semi-finals, although he was taking nothing for granted. 'If he's capable of beating Jim Courier, he's capable of beating me,' he said of the Russian. 'I'm not going to walk on court and think that because my name is John McEnroe that will be enough.'

On a day when Gary Lineker and Bobby Charlton were guests in the Royal Box, Boris Becker (a soccer fan) was outside on Court 2, still finding it difficult to achieve consistency on his serve as he beat American Bryan Shelton in four sets, and moved, no doubt with some misgivings, into a fourth-round match against the Queen's Club champion, Wayne Ferreira.

Further afield, on Court 14, there were always long queues waiting for a glimpse of Henri Leconte – no longer quite the clown prince of tennis but still just as entertaining – as he hoped to avenge the loss he had suffered in the equivalent round a year earlier, when his back let him down against fellow Frenchman, Guy Forget. It was not to be. The straight man beat the old joker, 7–6, 6–3, 3–6, 6–3. It was fine stuff to see.

The only problem came in trying to stay long enough at one match without missing something eventful and exciting somewhere else, such as three more seeds losing

in the ladies' singles, including Jana Novotna against the lively American, Patty Fendick.

Back on Centre Court, the crowd warmed to the diminutive Rika Hiraki, who suddenly found her range after taking a terrible drubbing in the first set, to give Gabriela Sabatini a reasonable match before the third seed won 6–0, 6–4. And then, as the sun began to drop, Steffi Graf became involved in a fascinating, lengthy struggle with South Africa's Mariaan de Swardt, 21, before continuing the defence of her title, after winning 5–7, 6–0, 7–5.

Just briefly, when Miss de Swardt broke the champion in the 11th game of the first set and delivered three boom-

ing serves on her way to taking it, there was the tantalizing prospect that the day's shocks might not have finished after all. But after a tough opening game of the second set, Miss Graf's game took off. She still had to work hard, not least after slipping and dropping the first point at 4–4 in the third, but with her serve and forehand in good order there was no longer any serious danger.

*Mariaan de Swardt (above) consistently served well to take a set from Steffi Graf.*

*Previous page: A loose shoelace – one of the familiar hazards for Jennifer Capriati.*

DAY

# 7

*Monday 29 June*

Providing the weather assists, the second Monday of The Championships is always likely to be one of the best. It is the day when the hopeful challengers are left behind by the serious contenders, as the line-up for the quarter-finals of both the men's and ladies' singles becomes known. This time, Day Seven was extra special, in as much as even the rest of the tennis world had started taking notice that, for the first time in a decade, a British player was still involved.

Yet although Jeremy Bates kept his promise to 'give everything I have to give', in the end there was only heart-break for the British number one, who came within a point of becoming the first Englishman to reach the quarter-finals since Yorkshire's Roger Taylor in 1973. Perhaps Bates's 6–7, 6–4, 3–6, 7–6, 6–3 defeat by Guy Forget was best summed up by the headline in the *Independent*, which read, 'Forget victorious but Bates unforgettable.'

Almost an hour after the hushed crowd, with Union Jacks at the ready, had been prepared to salute him as the winner, Bates instead found himself congratulating the ninth-seeded Frenchman on having achieved a quarter-final place against John McEnroe.

Three 'killer' net cords, one just before Bates reached his match point, another which cost him that game and a third during the fourth-set tie-break, all conspired to disappoint him and the crowd, more than any lack of courage or determination on his part, on Wimbledon's most scorchingly hot day for years.

Indeed, it was probably the first of those net cords – rather than the missed match point – that did the most damage, because it made the difference between Bates being 40–0, holding three match points, and being 30–15, still offering Forget a glimmer of hope. The tension at 40–30 could be felt not only within Centre Court but, once again, throughout the grounds of The All England Club, where several other matches were briefly halted as spectators following Bates's progress in sound, if not in vision, responded excitedly to what was happening.

As Bates prepared to serve on the match point he checked himself because the original toss was not right. 'Someone sneezed, I think,' he explained later. On the second serve, the delivery may have been a shade tentative and the arrival point a trifle short, but it was still a remarkable hit-or-miss return by the left-handed Frenchman that kept the game alive. It was bad enough for Bates when a second net cord then cost him the game, but that became cruelty beyond measure when, with Forget leading 3–2 in the tie-break, the tape decisively intervened again. The way Bates gestured as he changed ends, then 2–4 down, said it all. The backhand winner that Forget then drilled, with spectacular ferocity, on the next point simply rubbed salt into the wound.

*Overleaf: Guy Forget's elegant backhand winners came into their own against Jeremy Bates (right), who despite treatment from physiotherapist, John Matthews, could have done with a little more help from above.*

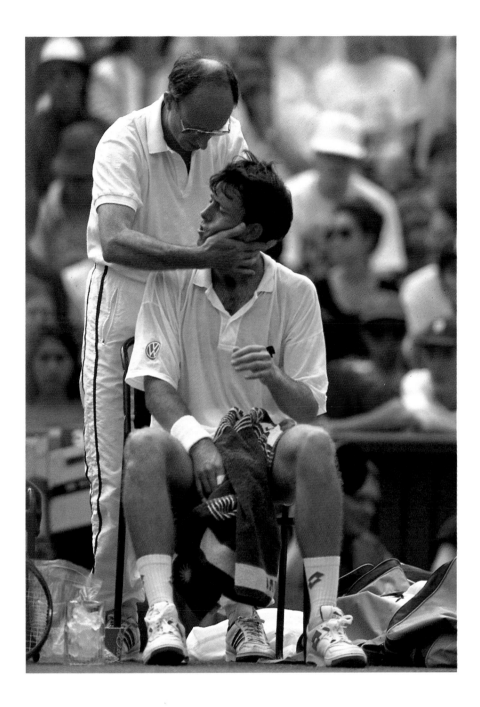

Forget hit 31 aces, the equivalent of almost eight games, prompting Bates, who had fought for every point, to reflect that if there was one thing he could add to his game, it would be a huge serve. With the mental crisis past, the quality, consistency and power of Forget's returns increased as well until, with four brilliant winners (two on either flank), he broke his opponent again in the ninth game of the final set.

'I knew I was almost out,' Forget said. 'But I still had a chance and I knew that if I could break back, then the pressure that I had been under would turn on him. You always need a bit of luck to win.' Then he added, 'I've always dreamed of playing someone like John McEnroe

on Centre Court.' In the event, his dream did not quite come true – when they met two days later it was on Court 1.

For his part, McEnroe looked even happier than the devoted supporters who were celebrating his victory, when he succeeded where Jim Courier had failed in beating Andrei Olhovskiy, to reach the last eight for only the second time in his last five visits.

Although there were only occasional flashes of the marvellous magic and inspiration so evident in his match against David Wheaton, McEnroe always seemed to have something in reserve as he beat the engaging Russian, 7–5, 6–3, 7–6. 'It was more of a grind than my last match,

*Stefan Edberg was still not entirely at ease in the fourth round against fellow Swede, Henrik Holm.*

*All good things come to an end. Qualifier Andrei Olhovskiy lost three exhausting sets on Court 2 against John McEnroe, who offered his victory salute sitting down.*

but it was also frustrating, because I always felt I had the chances but was never able really to take control,' he said, after being pressed to 12–10 before winning the third-set tie-break on his fifth match point.

Stefan Edberg, the second seed, beat fellow Swede, Henrik Holm, 6–3, 6–4, 6–7, 6–3, but once again lost his concentration when he should have been finishing the match off in the third set. He was broken to 15 while serving nervously at 6–5 and then, with his serve in disarray, lost a set for the first time in the tournament, 7–1 in the tie-break. 'I played a bad game. That's all I can say,' he commented.

If Bates felt he had a monopoly on bad luck that day, Ivan Lendl would probably have disagreed, although he was already trailing Goran Ivanisevic by two sets to one, and had just gone a break down in the fourth, when he told umpire Dana Loconto on Court 14 that a back injury meant he could not continue.

'He said last week his back was troubling him,' commented the Croatian. 'I don't know exactly what happened, but I could see in the middle of the first set that he was throwing the ball lower and was pretty slow moving to the net. I had a feeling that if I broke him early in the fourth set he would retire. And he did. He's a great athlete, a great tennis player but I knew a long time ago that he'd never win here. Grass isn't his game.'

André Agassi needed two tie-breaks to beat German qualifier, Christian Saceanu, on Court 2, but as he won both of them for the loss of only one point he was never seriously threatened in reaching the quarter-finals for a second consecutive year. Meanwhile Pete Sampras, again looking sharp on his serve – and even sharper on his returns – beat unseeded Arnaud Boetsch of France in straight sets.

Sampras produced 25 aces, prompting defending champion Michael Stich, his next opponent, to observe, 'He'll be very confident because he's so far played solidly in every round.' Stich once again started slowly, losing the first set of his match to Wally Masur, before overpowering the doughty Australian, and then at last completing his doubles victory with John McEnroe over defending champions John Fitzgerald and Anders Jarryd in a match left over from the previous Friday.

Once again, though, a match of major significance was left in limbo. Boris Becker and the impressive young South African, Wayne Ferreira, were locked in a thrilling, high-quality contest at two sets all when fading light meant that the last of the men's fourth-round matches had to be halted. It was 9.05 pm and the Centre Court was still filled almost to capacity when Ferreira, 20, struck a scorching double-handed backhand service return to win the fourth-set tie-break 8–6, three points after one of his

*Arnaud Boetsch was outgunned by Pete Sampras.*

*A typical tumble for Boris Becker, who had saved his best for last against Wayne Ferreira.*

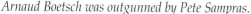

*Martina Navratilova was her usual sprightly self in curbing Yayuk Basuki.*

serves had denied Becker a match point.

Ferreira had taken the first set but Becker, serving well, took the next two and had served for the match at 5–4 in the gathering gloom, only to be broken to 30. 'It's his own fault that he has to come back to finish it off tomorrow,' said his manager, Ion Tiriac.

By contrast, the fourth-round matches in the ladies' singles were all reasonably straightforward, even though Steffi Graf again dropped a first set – this time against Patty Fendick. And there was one seeding upset when Natalia Zvereva maintained her return to form by beating 1990 runner-up, Zina Garrison, 6–2, 3–6, 6–1, with a shrewd mixture of drop shots and sizzling groundstrokes.

It was the tenacious serve-and-volley tactics of Miss Fendick that tested Miss Graf's nerve long into the evening again, and it was not until midway through the second set that the former world champion's match-winning forehand once again switched itself on to ensure a 4–6, 6–3, 6–2 victory.

The only other seed to drop a set was Jennifer Capriati, who went through another of her increasingly familiar

and dangerous roller-coaster performances before beating Japan's Naoko Sawamatsu on Court 2. The young American had taken the first set comfortably enough, but then her concentration deserted her, and from 2–0 she lost the next five games, littering the scene with unforced errors. There was another lapse in the final set when a 3–0 lead suddenly became a 3–4 deficit, but Miss Sawamatsu then suffered from a combination of fatigue and nerves, as Miss Capriati finished strongly.

Gigi Fernandez exactly doubled the number of games she had accumulated from two previous matches against Monica Seles when she lost 6–4, 6–2, in a match when the grunting became louder as the top seed's driving became harder. Miss Seles also won admirers for conceding a point to her opponent when Miss Fernandez disagreed with a linesman's call. 'I only do it if I know a call is wrong and my opponent is right in questioning the decision,' Miss Seles said.

When it was put to her that not all of today's players might respond in such a generous fashion, she explained that it was all to do with her love of tennis. 'I don't look at the money. In fact I don't even know what the winner

wins here. I just look at the game and get my fun from playing each point.'

Martina Navratilova cruised through her match 7–5, 6–2, once she had overcome stylish, as well as stubborn, first-set resistance from Yayuk Basuki. One by one, with the exception of Miss Zvereva, the eight unseeded players who had begun the day (all facing seeds) were thus left behind. In the bottom half of the draw, Gabriela Sabatini ended a memorable time for Kristin Godridge – who had beaten ninth-seeded Manuela Maleeva-Fragniere in the previous round – by beating the Australian, 6–2, 6–1. From now on, the real battles in the ladies' singles would begin.

*Jennifer Capriati (above) could hardly believe how some chances slipped away.*

*Opposite: First-round disappointment in the juniors for Britain's Amanda Wainwright against Czechoslovakia's Zuzano Nemsakova.*

The completion of one match that had been left unfinished overnight and the near-completion of another provided the highlights of Day Eight, when the weather had to be blamed for taking some of the spotlight away from the ladies' quarter-finals.

Because of the first rain of the fortnight, it was 5.13 pm before Boris Becker hit the first ball of the day on Centre Court at the start of an awesome 29-minute set, in which he booked his delayed quarter-final place at the expense of Wayne Ferreira. It was 9.01 pm when Jennifer Capriati hit the last ball of the day and convinced officials that Gabriela Sabatini should be kept waiting overnight before being allowed to try and serve out the one extra game she needed to join the other ladies among the top four seeds – Monica Seles, Steffi Graf and Martina Navratilova – in the semi-finals.

In between, the most significant development of the day had been the view of the French player, Nathalie Tauziat, that it was not only the relentless power of the Seles groundstrokes that were too much for her but also that famous, and now officially infamous, grunt. According to the Women's Tennis Association, Miss Tauziat's request to New Zealand umpire David Crymble for Miss Seles to tone down the noise was the first time such a request had been made during any tournament.

Miss Tauziat, the 14th seed, was however at pains to stress that the 'big screams', as she called them, could not be blamed for her 6–1, 6–3 defeat in 55 minutes. 'I lost because she's better than me, not because she made so much noise, but sometimes it disturbs you more than others,' she said. 'And the longer the point lasted, the louder it became, so that I couldn't hear the ball as it came off her racket, which is important.'

Miss Seles refused to be drawn into the controversy except to insist, as she had done all along, that she was still genuinely trying to kick the habit. But clearly one habit she had no intention of kicking was her penchant for fierce, double-handed backhands, especially crosscourt, although her first major test was still to come – against Martina Navratilova.

The nine-times champion secured her 108th singles victory at the tournament she loves most with a 6–3, 7–6 defeat of Katerina Maleeva, who volleyed more than most had expected from this classic baseliner. Indeed, it was Miss Maleeva who broke first in a fascinating second set, which was fittingly settled in the tie-break when Miss Navratilova's spring-heeled approach reasserted itself as she took a commanding 5–0 lead. Few could have disagreed with Miss Navratilova's assessment, either then or, even more so, during the semi-finals, that 'I'm fitter at thirty-five than most players are in their twenties. Age is a state of mind, and I'm defying it as well as

*Total concentration from Martina Navratilova as she reached the semi-finals.*

*A new partnership but instantly successful – for John McEnroe and Michael Stich.*

I possibly can,' she continued. 'Should Van Gogh have stopped painting at a certain age?'

There was nothing quite so romantic about the way Steffi Graf accounted for Natalia Zvereva, beating her 6–3, 6–1 in 55 minutes. The Russian, who had already knocked out two seeds, could not cope with Miss Graf's now well-grooved forehand, and once she was broken in the third game of the second set it was all just a formality.

The best of the ladies' quarter-finals was undoubtedly the last. Miss Sabatini, varying her shots well and making full use of the court, romped through the first set 6–1. But Miss Capriati's spirits suddenly soared after she broke for 3–1 in the second and, although broken back, she then benefited from Miss Sabatini's double fault in the eighth game.

Miss Capriati would have liked the match stopped for the night then, but the light was actually brighter then than it had been a few games earlier. With Miss Sabatini taking a 3–0 lead in the deciding set, as the Capriati errors once more began to outnumber the winners – she lost eleven points in succession – it seemed as if it would anyway soon be over. But for an incredible point at 5–2 and deuce, when Capriati played a winning stop volley, it probably would have been. Instead Capriati, who had again appealed unsuccessfully for the match to be halted

at the start of the eighth game, held for 3–5 before the players were eventually taken off, with the Argentinian just four points from victory.

Back, though, to Becker. That one set he played to complete a 3–6, 6–3, 6–4, 6–7, 6–1 victory over Ferreira was one of the most brilliantly stunning that he, or anyone else, had played at Wimbledon since he last won the title in 1989. For someone with the reputation of being a notoriously slow starter, he had started in a hurry and gone on to win like a hurricane. 'My form is coming good just at the right time,' he claimed. Then, looking forward to his clash the next day with André Agassi, he said, 'If I play like that, André will have to work hard to win.'

There was nothing remotely gentle about Becker's start. He held to 15, then immediately broke Ferreira to love, helped by two crunching returns off the forehand and another two off the backhand. 'At 2–0 it was easier to play. I felt I was pretty much in control,' he said.

On a day when Becker hit many shots worthy of a champion, one in particular stood out – the fabulous backhand pass down the line after Ferreira had played a challenging volley to the baseline. The South African, who had shown when winning the Stella Artois title at Queen's Club that he can be as cool as he is accomplished, was broken to 5–1. Becker's win also produced a quarter-final line-up which, for the first time since 1928, included four champions – himself, Edberg, McEnroe and the holder, Stich. Sixty-four years earlier, Henri Cochet, René Lacoste, Jean Borotra and Bill Tilden had shared the distinction.

The Becker-Ferreira match was certainly explosive stuff, and a just reward for those spectators who had waited with typical stoicism for the rain – which had started at 12.47 pm, just when everything was in full swing on the outside courts – to move away.

Before taking their seats on Centre Court, some fans had doubtless been on Courts 2 and 3, watching the now gentle but still wonderfully attractive skills of old favourites such as Ilie Nastase and Tom Okker against John Newcombe and Tony Roche, or John Cooper and Neale Fraser against Bob Hewitt and Frew McMillan, the latter still wearing a cap – though not, he assured questioners, the original one.

While Becker still had singles business to deal with, the prime occupation for McEnroe and Stich that evening was to continue to improve the doubles harmony they had established at Rosmalen a couple of weeks earlier. Their opponents in the third round were two American heavyweights, Kent Kinnear and Sven Salumaa, both 25, both 14st 3lb and standing 6ft 5in. Though such physical advantages had been too much for the British pair, Chris Bailey and Chris Wilkinson, in the first round, the combination of McEnroe's touch and Stich's power was this time too much for the Americans. The unseeded favourites won 6–3, 6–2, 6–4.

Meanwhile, although Jeremy Bates and Jo Durie (former holders of the mixed doubles title) were bowing out against the eighth seeds, Holland's Tom Nijssen and Manon Bollegraf, 6–4, 7–6 in the third round, encouraging British results were being recorded by some of the juniors, especially Lancashire's Barry Cowan. For the second successive day he beat an opponent ranked far above him, eliminating the 15th seed, Filip Kascak of Czechoslovakia, 7–5, 6–1, to reach the last 16.

# DAY 9

## *Wednesday 1 July*

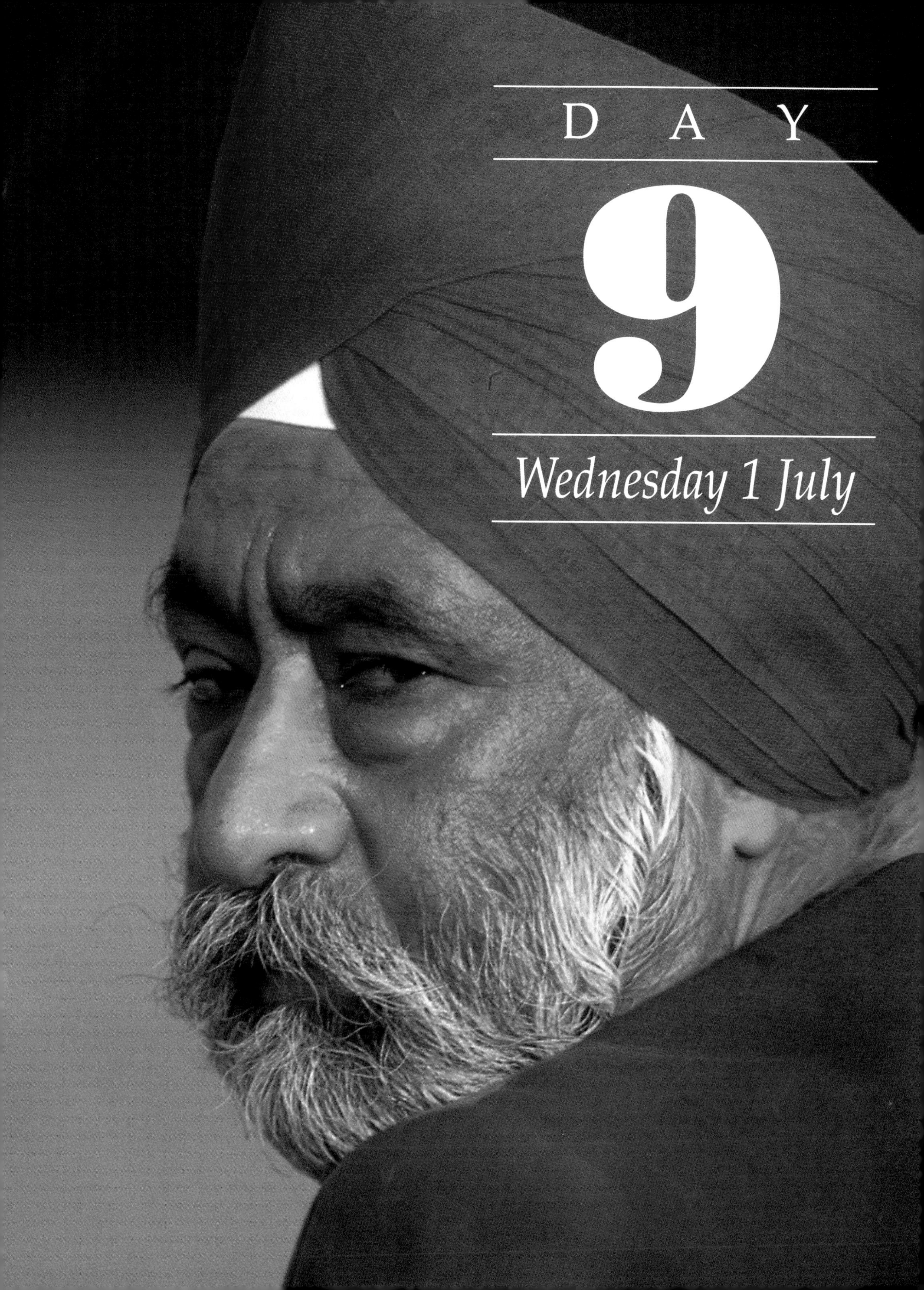

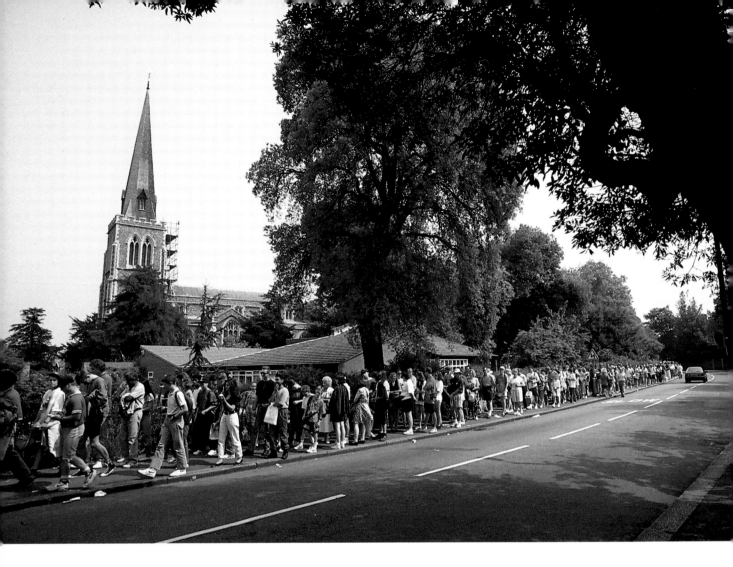

Day Nine, which began with the fascinating possibility that four champions might reach the semi-finals, was another ended prematurely by the weather, with two of the champions beaten and the other two facing an anxious wait overnight.

Michael Stich had lost his crown and Stefan Edberg, his predecessor, the chance to succeed him by the time the rain abbreviated what was shaping up to be another classic chapter in Wimbledon's history. Boris Becker was two sets to one down and fighting desperately for survival against André Agassi, when the elements provided him with the opportunity he needed to take stock. And John McEnroe was locked at 5–5 in the second set against the Frenchman, Guy Forget, after producing vintage tennis in taking the first set, to the delight of the Court 1 crowd.

In between, Gabriela Sabatini took 143 seconds to win the four points of the one game she needed to complete a 6–1, 3–6, 6–3 defeat of Jennifer Capriati, which had been left in limbo from the night before. Indeed the action, confined to three errors by Miss Capriati and one splendid volley by the Argentinian, lasted less than half the time of the warm-up.

*Pete Sampras steadfastly considers his next move on the way to beating the defending champion, Michael Stich.*

*Previous page: One of Wimbledon's longest-serving court officials.*

*Determination in every sinew as Goran Ivanisevic hits 33 aces to beat former champion, Stefan Edberg.*

Miss Sabatini's victory, which gave her the confidence to suggest that she now had a good enough game to beat Steffi Graf (her semi-final opponent) on grass, also guaranteed the presence of the top four seeds in the semi-finals of the ladies' singles. The same had been true at the French Open in Paris a month earlier, and it was the 12th time it had happened at Wimbledon since seeding was introduced in 1927.

This, however, was just a brief interlude between an outstanding display by Pete Sampras against Stich and the arrival of Agassi and Becker. If the style and scale of Sampras's 6–3, 6–2, 6–4 victory over the defending champion were astonishing, the outcome itself was not. Despite Sampras's failure to go beyond the second round in the previous three years, one felt that it was only a matter of time before he started to approach the target he had set himself (when he switched from a double-handed to a single-handed backhand at the age of 14) of becoming 'a right-handed Rod Laver'.

Hitherto Sampras's problems at Wimbledon had been not so much with his serve, as with his returns. He had spent most of the week before the 1992 Championships concentrating on this aspect of his game under the direction of his coach, Tim Gullikson. 'That's making the difference,' he said, after overwhelming Stich on an afternoon when the often disgruntled German found fault with the court, the line-calls and, above all, his own form.

Yet while Sampras went off happily declaring, 'I'm not satisfied by any means; I came here to win the tournament and that's what I'm trying to do', the philosophical Stich admitted, 'He killed me out there. He played perfect grass-court tennis. But I shall always be the 1991 Wimbledon champion. Nobody can take that away from me.'

Goran Ivanisevic had estimated beforehand that he would probably need 40 aces to be sure of beating Edberg to take his place opposite Sampras in the semi-finals. In the event, 33 were enough, prompting the Swede to say, 'He hits the serve with so much power. If he stays that way it's going to be difficult for anyone to beat him.'

The score was 6–7, 7–5, 6–1, 3–6, 6–3, and the nearer he advanced to victory, the more excited Ivanisevic became, until at his second match point – when Edberg's misdirected backhand flew over the baseline – he offered the most exaggerated of clench-fisted salutes.

Ivanisevic, a lean, lanky left-hander, has never lacked talent. Temperament has always been his problem, and he tells the story of how, early in 1991, he watched a video of himself playing and suddenly realized, 'I saw me complaining too much.'

Since then, and with considerable help from coach Bob Brett, he has striven to eradicate such a wasteful streak,

*Perhaps Boris Becker is right when he says he knows every inch of the Centre Court turf.*

although for someone with such an emotional personality, the pressures on him from home have not made it easy. 'I want to win Wimbledon for Croatia,' he explained. 'That would be a nice gift. I just hope they are going to finish that war and let the people lead normal lives.'

Although Edberg won the opening set in a 12–10 tie-break, after five set points had been alternatively saved, he had to wait until late in the fourth set for his next break point. But the decisive moment came in the eighth game of the final set, when Ivanisevic benefited from two net cords, the second at 30–40. At that moment Edberg knew exactly how Jeremy Bates had felt 48 hours earlier, although he still made one last, valiant attempt to break back, twice reaching break point only to be denied the game by Ivanisevic's 33rd ace and another unreturnable serve.

*Guy Forget was already under growing pressure from John McEnroe when rain halted play overnight.*

'Last year,' said Ivanisevic afterwards, 'if I hit one or two bad shots, I was finished. Now I am concentrating great; strong in my mind. I'm in the semi-final again and I'll fight every ball. This time we'll see.' On his first semi-final two years earlier he reflected, 'That was like going to the cinema for me, you know. I had great fun being there but I didn't believe I could win.'

The trouble with Wimbledon is that there is usually so much you want to see that you know you are bound to miss something. This was another occasion when spectators on Centre Court would at times have loved to have been on Court 1 as well – and vice-versa – or, best of all, in both places at the same time. That was especially so for those on Centre Court during the early stages of the Becker-Agassi clash, which was played to the regular accompaniment of shrieks and cheers as Ivanisevic on Court 1 moved closer to beating Edberg.

'What's that?' Becker asked umpire John Parry after one particularly loud shout from next door. 'The other court,' he was told. 'Sounds like a good match – can I go and have a look?' Then Agassi, who was waiting to serve at 2–0 in the second set at the time, joined in by dropping his racket on the baseline, leaving it there and walking to the umpire's chair, requesting, 'Can I go too?'

In a year when there had been so much discussion about the dominance of the serve in men's tennis, Agassi was clearly moving towards the sort of form on his service returns that would provide the perfect antidote. The opening set, in which Becker clung to a service break from a fine forehand cross-court pass in the seventh game, gave little hint of the barnstorming response to come. But the American looked in irrepressible mood as he established a 2–1 lead in sets with one of those astonishing, carefree displays of big hitting that are more usually associated with a practice session.

Agassi's appetite for countering Becker's pace and power was voracious, and the manner of it explosively entertaining, not least because of the colossal, competing personalities of the two players involved. It was only when, probably inevitably, the range and timing of Agassi's shots faltered a little – and the three-times former champion took advantage of this and at least came within sight of levelling the match in the fourth set – that play was abandoned for the day. By then the match had lasted 2 hours 24 minutes and Becker was 4–3 ahead in the fourth set and about to serve, when the first sighting of those colourful golf umbrellas preceded the arrival of torrential rain.

If Ivanisevic's fiery temper is now being channelled into more productive avenues, then the presentation of John McEnroe's still-vigorous complaints has at least mellowed over the years. So he demonstrated when, not

*Oxfordshire's Lizzie Jelfs, a late replacement in the draw, lost a tough second round against Ai Sugiyama, 8–6 in the third set of the juniors' singles.*

*Overleaf: 'Do you mind if we pop next door for a moment, it sounds quite exciting,' say Boris Becker and André Agassi, as the cheers mount with Goran Ivanisevic close to beating Stefan Edberg.*

for the first time, he ran foul of Cyclops, the service-line monitor, just as his quarter-final with Forget was moving into a critical phase.

McEnroe, who had won the first set 6–2 with a series of fine winners, was at 2–2 in the second when there was a dispute over whether a Forget serve had been a fault (as the bleep indicated) or an ace (as declared by the linesman and umpire George Grime). McEnroe immediately disputed the decision, but there was none of the 'You cannot be serious' stuff of old. 'How can you sit there pontificating like that?' was his offering this time, before he was forced to retreat, wounded in as much as he had lost the argument, but successful in that the machine was switched off for the remaining five games before, at 5–5, everyone had to take cover.

Away from the singles, the most important action in the restricted doubles play saw the defeat of mixed doubles holders John Fitzgerald and Liz Smylie, 6–2, 7–6, by Jim Pugh and Natalia Zvereva in the second round.

Meanwhile, Luke Jensen continued to attract large crowds – fascinated by his ability to be ambidextrous, not only on groundstrokes but also on serve – as he and Jennifer Capriati advanced to round three with a 6–2, 7–6 defeat of Todd Nelson and Gretchen Magers.

Among the juniors, British interest was importantly maintained as Miles MacLagen, volleying well to overcome Argentine's Lucas Arnold 6–3, 7–6, joined Barry Cowan in the last 16 of the boys' singles. And Shirli-Ann Siddall became the sole home representative through to the same stage of the girls' event when she beat Thailand's Siriluk Mingmolee, 6–1, 6–1.

*Left: Luke Jensen. Opponents never know whether to expect a right-handed or left-handed serve.*

*Above: Dorset's Shirli-Ann Siddall surged through to the third round of the junior girls.*

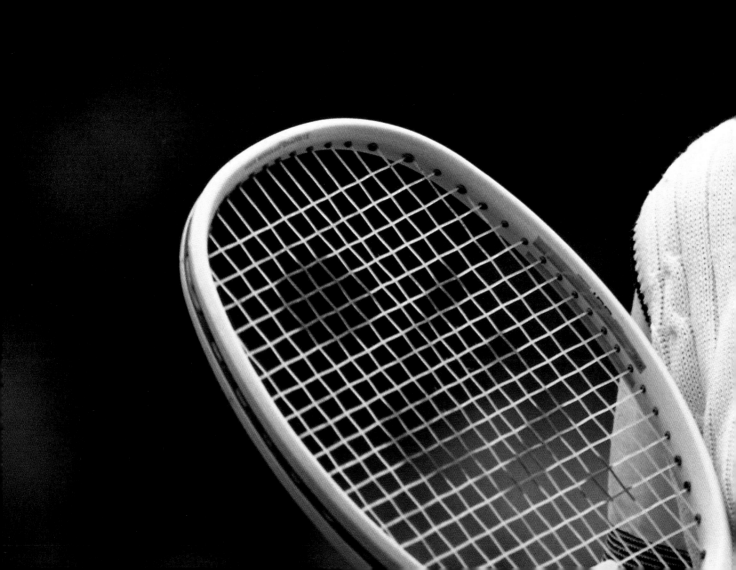

DAY

# 10

*Thursday 2 July*

There was, of course, major unfinished business to be completed before the traditional highlight of this day could begin – the semi-finals of the ladies' singles. Those two remaining quarter-finals in the men's singles still had to be resolved.

Back on Day Two of The Championships, as he looked forward with relish to playing fellow former champion, Pat Cash, John McEnroe had jokingly said of his chances of winning the title again, 'You can't totally discount me if two or three guys break their legs, someone gets struck by lightning or something. But I suppose I've a better chance than most in the draw.'

Metaphorically speaking, the way Jim Courier had been removed from McEnroe's path was probably akin to being struck by lightning. Otherwise, there was no doubt – after McEnroe completed his 6–2, 7–6, 6–3, increasingly straightforward victory over Guy Forget – that the old warrior, now 33, greying, balding, but still totally competitive, deserved to be in the semi-finals. He would be unseeded again, just as he had been on his first visit, as a qualifier, 15 years earlier.

Resuming their match at 5–5, the second set that had been suspended overnight quickly reached a tie-break, during which McEnroe not only recovered from 3–6 after a disputed call gave the Frenchman three set points, but from three more – one of them with the most perfectly disguised lob. Finally, on his own first set point, McEnroe's ferocious backhand return forced Forget to net the volley.

While McEnroe had climbed another step up the ladder towards the fulfilment of his dream – 'there's a little voice somewhere inside me which keeps telling me I can do it,' the American revealed – Forget, who had clearly used up all his luck against Jeremy Bates, pined, 'It was mine and I let it go. Although I continued to have chances in the third set, in my mind I knew I'd lost the match in the tie-break.'

It took Agassi, just as convinced in his own mind as Monica Seles that baseliners can win Wimbledon, 50 minutes to complete his 4–6, 6–2, 6–2, 4–6, 6–3 defeat of Becker. 'Being in the semi-final here means more to me than being in the final of any other Grand Slam. This place gives you an energy like none other,' he said.

That was quite apparent as Agassi, despite losing the fourth set, in which he had been 4–3 down overnight, then resumed the spectacular flow of groundstroke winners that destroyed Becker for a sixth consecutive time. 'There's only a few people who show up at Wimbledon who really come here to win it, and I'm one of them,' he commented. 'Goran's the only one left I haven't beaten, so I consider my chance is as good as anybody's.'

Becker's defeat, which ended his record of having

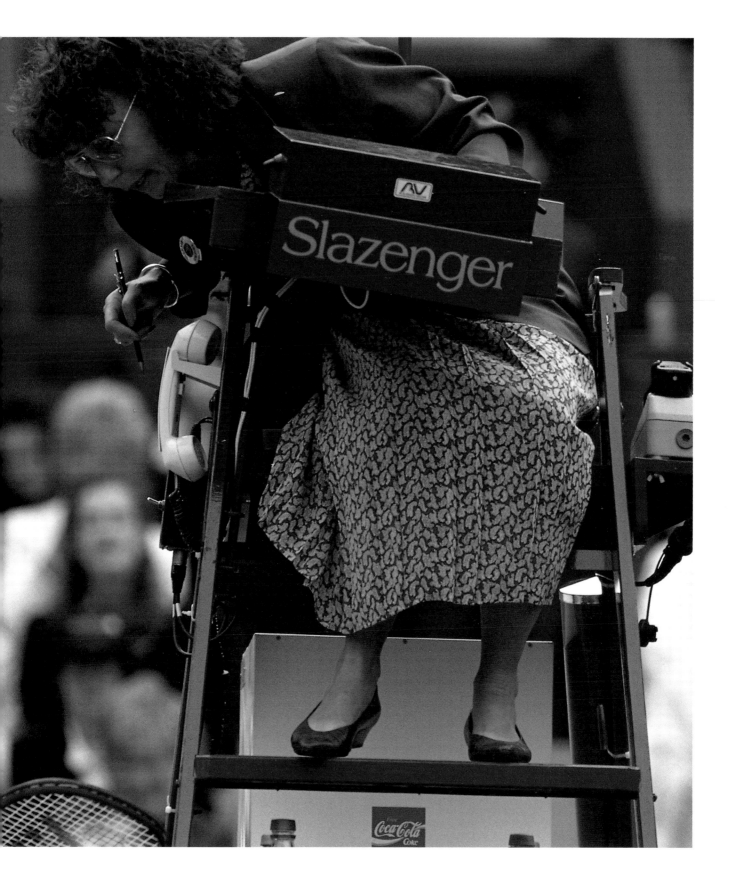

In the end the going was just too tough for Martina
Navratilova (previous page) after a brilliant match with
Monica Seles, who discovered that when umpire Fran

McDowell was asking for 'quiet, please' it included her, as
well as the crowd.

reached the final six times in the previous seven years, was not entirely a surprise – and not only because Agassi could really claim to have his number. Despite that one awesome set Becker had produced against Wayne Ferreira, it was predictable that sooner or later his lack of match practice – only 11 singles matches between February and the start of Wimbledon – albeit mostly because of injury, would take its toll.

Not that Becker, who did not play badly, quite saw it that way. He reassured himself with the thought that 'He [Agassi] plays the whole year not so great and then he sees my face and he plays his best. He hit some shots that are not even in the book. I haven't seen anyone play from the back on grass like that.'

The wins for Agassi (seeded 12) and McEnroe (not seeded at all) meant that for the first time since 1951 not one of the top four seeds had reached the semi-finals. It also gave the Americans three representatives at this exciting stage of the tournament for the first time since 1982, when McEnroe's compatriots on that occasion had been Jimmy Connors and Tim Mayotte.

At last the stage was cleared for the ladies to take over. When they did so, Steffi Graf struck her forehand with even more energy than a troubled Monica Seles put into her grunting, as the two best players in the world reached what almost everyone – bar Gabriela Sabatini and Martina Navratilova, of course – regarded as the perfect final.

Miss Graf's 6–3, 6–3 defeat of Miss Sabatini was as clinically efficient as the defending champion would have wished it to be, spiced also by the greater variety of shots she was willing to risk, now that her self-belief had been restored. It mattered little to her that, as a match, it fell some way short of the excitement generated by Miss Seles and Miss Navratilova.

Indeed, it is doubtful whether anyone other than Miss Graf at her very best, or Miss Seles, could have countered the wonderfully determined and skilful challenge presented by the veteran nine-times champion, before she eventually went down 6–2, 6–7, 6–4. Not for years had the 35-year-old Miss Navratilova maintained such a sustained and compelling grass-court display and yet, when the crunch came in a gripping final set, she could not quite counter her opponent's greater weight of shot.

Twice Miss Navratilova broke back and had the chance to draw level but each time Monica Seles, ever more determined and, noticeably, ever more noisy, broke straight back – the mark of a true champion. 'A couple of times it was just the pace of her ball that beat me,' Miss Navratilova admitted. 'At the French [where Miss Seles recovered from 2–4 in the final set against Miss Sabatini] she played great when she was down. She wasn't down

*Barry Cowan from Lancashire – much stylish promise in defeat, in the third round of the junior boys' singles.*

today but she still turned it up a notch.'

Sadly for Miss Navratilova, joyous moments – such as the blistering forehand with which she rounded off an exciting rally while breaking back to 3–4, and the perfectly placed lob when she broke back again to 4–5 – were spoiled by one or two of those horrendous volley errors that would never have occurred a few years ago. Yet with hindsight, Miss Navratilova will probably reflect most earnestly over the fifth game of the final set, when she missed three chances to break for 3–2 at a time when her opponent was beginning to look distinctly unsettled. She had struck a superb sliced forehand approach, but although Miss Seles's return would have been easy for her to put away at the net, she let it go and then looked horrified to see the ball drop in.

Like Nathalie Tauziat one round earlier, Miss Navratilova felt obliged, first at 2–2 in the second set and again during the third, to ask American umpire, Fran McDowell, if her opponent could tone down the grunting. 'It just gets louder and louder so you can't hear the ball being hit, which you need to,' she insisted, accepting the assurance from Miss Seles that it was not done on purpose, but countering, 'She can stop doing it on purpose.'

Sadly it was this, rather than the magnificence of the match, which occupied much of the discussion in the interview room later. Miss Navratilova, who had already said, 'Grunting or not, she's a great player', was angered when asked why, after playing Miss Seles ten times, she had never complained about it before. 'Am I on trial here or is her grunting on trial? You sound like I am making sour grapes. I only complained when I was winning...It's unbelievable. If I don't say anything, I'm damned; if I do, I'm damned. It's catch twenty-two.'

Those hoping to see a Graf-Sabatini spectacle similar to the previous year's final, in which Miss Sabatini served – or perhaps it should be said, failed successfully to serve – for the match before losing a final set 8–6, may have been disappointed. Miss Graf's strong serve and booming forehand groundstrokes simply proved too much for her Argentinian rival. Compensation came with the spectacular sight of Miss Graf recapturing her most devastating form, as displayed during her Grand Slam in 1988, at the most appropriate moment.

Miss Sabatini, who had won 11 of their 32 previous meetings, including the only two since their final 12 months earlier, hailed her opponent's performance as 'one of the best I've ever seen'. Miss Graf was in control from the moment she broke Miss Sabatini to love in the fourth game, and she coasted through the first set in 30 minutes, losing only five points on her serve. Braver resistance from Miss Sabatini in the second set ended after the

*Life at the top can be tough – even for Monica Seles.*

*Steffi Graf's game really took off as she pounded many forehand winners to beat Gabriela Sabatini.*

seventh game, when a delicate lob for the break sent the German skipping to the chair 4–3 up, and safe in the belief that her own serve was not likely to be threatened.

Some compensation for Miss Navratilova after her heroic singles effort came when she and Pam Shriver, still chasing records in the ladies' doubles, moved into the semi-finals with a 6–3, 6–1 defeat of Australian Jo-Anne Faull and New Zealander Julie Richardson. Indeed, as in the singles, the top four seeds all reached their appointed places in the last four, including the 1991 champions, Larisa Savchenko-Neiland and Natalia Zvereva, now playing with different partners – Jana Novotna and Gigi Fernandez respectively, who together had been runners-up a year earlier. A case of mixed-up doubles, perhaps.

In the men's doubles, Forget put his singles defeat behind him when he and Jakob Hlasek beat Scott Davis and David Pate over five lively sets. Meanwhile McEnroe and Stich continued their impressive progress with a 6–3, 6–4, 6–4 quarter-final defeat of the Dutch pair, Paul Haarhuis (who had knocked the American out of the US Open in 1989) and Mark Koevermans.

Yet the doubles with the most appeal on this second

Thursday came unexpectedly – but none the less joyously – when, as an extra treat (unannounced until the last moment), four great names from the past, John Newcombe and Tony Roche, Frew McMillan and Bob Hewitt, walked on to Centre Court.

Many of the spectators who were about to leave duly changed their minds. And how sensible they were. For the next hour or so they were treated to pure, brilliant nostalgia as – admittedly at a slower pace and with less power than in the old days – the four produced a wonderful display of beautiful angles, drop shots, lobs and the occasional firm drive, amid much good humour and banter during and between points.

Once, when a shot was flying well beyond the baseline, McMillan dived, like a slip fielder, to catch it. Sometimes, after missing a volley, Hewitt resurrected his cheerful trick of throwing back another ball that he had been holding, to pretend he had hit a winner after all. Although there were two chairs for them on either side of the umpire, these were used only for hanging their clothes on.

Apart from perhaps 20 seconds while they sipped a

drink and dried their hands, the players walked straight round at the change-overs, just as it used to be – and just as many would still like it to be. The Centre Court stayed almost full, especially the Members' Stand, and, although the score was a one-sided 6–1, 6–2 for the Australians, the three- to four-minute standing ovation at the end said 'thanks for the memory' to all concerned.

To round off an exhilarating day, Miles MacLagan became the first British player to reach the quarter-finals of the junior singles since Chris Bailey in 1986, when he beat Zambian-born Olivier Tauma of France, 7–5, 6–3, after saving three break points that followed three double faults in the fifth game.

On the debit side, Barry Cowan's encouraging week ended when he was overwhelmed by the power of the giant top seed, Grant Doyle from Australia, 6–2, 6–2. And Shirli-Ann Siddall never recovered from losing 13 of the first 15 points as she went down 6–3, 6–0 to Israel's Russian-born Anna Smashnova, the fifth seed.

# D A Y

# 11

*Friday 3 July*

# 12

*Saturday 4 Ju*

*Previous page: Pete Sampras found heavy serving was not enough against Goran Ivanisevic.*

In recent years, the Women's Tennis Association has generously provided a gift to those competing at Wimbledon. In 1991, when the incessant rain made it the wettest fortnight in the history of The Championships, they chose an umbrella. This year, when the second week bore the brunt of the bad weather, it was a rain suit.

Those unlucky enough to have experienced only the 10th day to be fully washed out since 1914, when they had been expecting to enjoy the semi-finals of the men's singles, will be hoping that the WTA offers sun-glasses and sun lotions instead in the future.

Apart from one brief spell in mid-afternoon when the Centre Court covers were removed, but then smartly restored within a few minutes, the rain fell steadily for much of the day until at 5.30 pm the 'no play' decision was taken. Christopher Gorringe, Chief Executive of The All England Club, expressing everyone's disappointment, said they would 'like to thank everyone for being so patient'.

Not to be denied some entertainment, however, many in the crowd joined stewards, umpires, policemen and the ball boys and girls in making some of their own, and for a while it was almost like the previous year's Middle Sunday as, both on Centre Court and Court 1, everyone let their hair down.

When they were not singing in the rain, they were dancing in the stands instead. One Sergeant in the Royal Greenjackets, whose name was not given for security reasons, led the way with renderings of 'Mona Lisa', 'Bye Bye Blackbird' and 'Heart of my Heart'. Meanwhile Lance-Corporal Dean Wheeler from the 2nd Royal Tank Regiment, working as a steward, used a golf umbrella as a baton to conduct a general sing-song. Later he led them in a hokey-cokey and a conga. Not to be outdone, the umpires and line judges came up with song-and-dance routines of their own, at least bringing some fun and smiles to the depressing scene.

The rearranged schedule that this entailed meant that inadvertently Wimbledon was to have, for the first time, its own version of the US Open's 'Super Saturday', except that at Flushing Meadow the ladies' singles final slots in between the two semi-finals of the men's singles. Wimbledon's answer was to try and be fair to everyone by staging the two men's matches simultaneously on Centre Court and Court 1 at 11.30 am, with Steffi Graf v Monica Seles to follow on Centre Court, but not before the traditional time of 2 pm. In the event, Agassi's brilliance meant that the men did their bit by vacating the stage on time, but then the showers returned to create more interruptions and delays on what became 'soggy Saturday'.

Surprise, surprise, McEnroe's first problem when he

and his Davis Cup colleague began their semi-final, watched by (among others) The Archbishop of Canterbury and Bruce Forsyth, was the sun in his eyes when preparing to serve. Yet it was not long before the 33-year-old American, hoping that his 200th match in Grand Slam tournaments would propel him into his sixth Wimbledon final, discovered that Agassi's power off the ground was dazzling him even more than the sun.

McEnroe, the oldest of all the four semi-finalists by eleven years, increasingly felt every day of that handicap as Agassi, hitting groundstrokes with enormous power, confidence and control, operated his forehand like a piledriver, for a 6–4, 6–2, 6–3 victory.

The old campaigner, who knew he needed to serve particularly well and consistently to curb Agassi's blistering returns, was actually in trouble on his serve from the first game, which he lost with a double fault. And there were other double faults that undermined him still further. His second, for instance, gave Agassi the break that enabled him to serve out for the opening set, prompting McEnroe, with a look of despair, to toss away his racket. The next three double faults maintained the

*'I've paid for my seat so I'm sitting in it.'*

*Overleaf: The brilliance of André Agassi left John McEnroe in torment but they remained good friends.*

self-inflicted pattern. One carried Agassi to break point in the opening game of the second set; the others helped the young contender to break for 5–2, and then again for 1–0 in the third.

Yet the double faults were really a reflection of the unrelenting pressure that McEnroe felt against an opponent who – unless the first serve was deep and penetrating – all too often used him for target practice. Often McEnroe was left, hands on hips, lips pursed, pondering on shots that had passed him, and no doubt wondering whether they would have done so a few years ago. Although those wonderfully explosive, dipping double-handed crosscourt winners from the backhand were the most prolific in Agassi's armoury, there was even one single-handed backhand down the line to savour.

When McEnroe, having lost seven consecutive games, held his serve for 1–2 in the third set, he raised his arms aloft in mock triumph. For most of the time he was so powerless to turn the tide, however, that his occasional expressions of dissent never reached a scale that might have required Madam Speaker, Betty Boothroyd, watch-

ing from the Royal Box, to call for 'Order'.

Just once, when from 40–0 Agassi was pulled back to deuce, serving for 5–3 in the final set, he might have wavered. He still has the reputation of having allowed too many of his most important matches to slip away, but he remained secure and that point heartened Nick Bollettieri, his coach for nine years, more than any other. 'That's the first time I've seen him get to a pressure point in a Grand Slam tournament and get through it,' he said. 'I think the hump is off his shoulder and that he's now capable of winning.'

And of those spectacular groundstrokes that Agassi struck in a match lasting 1 hour 51 minutes, Bollettieri (who is as flamboyant as his most successful player) commented, 'When God gives you hands and eyes like that, something has to happen eventually. He's had a tough year and to see him enjoying himself and performing again means a lot to me, because I don't like to see him in the sort of agony he's been through.'

As for Agassi, who had returned home after losing in Paris and hardly practised at all, let alone on grass, until arriving in London 72 hours before Wimbledon began,

*Above: Former champion Chris Evert leans out from the NBC commentary booth to check if it is still raining for fellow commentators Bud Collins (left) and Dick Emberg.*

*Left: The umpires do their Gene Kelly bit – singing . . . and dancing in the rain.*

*Overleaf: Steffi Graf (right) was quickly back into her stride against Monica Seles in the ladies' final once the covers came off.*

he continued his very personal style of progress by declaring, 'I'm at a loss for words . . . ' and then went on to prove, in exuberant fashion, that he most certainly was not.

Going into the other semi-final on Court 1, Pete Sampras and Goran Ivanisevic had hit 220 aces between them. What promised, or even threatened, to be a long serving stalemate, especially when they split the first two sets on tie-breaks, ended when Sampras buckled, so destroying the American hope that Independence Day might inspire an all-American final 24 hours later.

For the first 105 minutes there was little respite from the crash-bang-wallop, serve and first volley routine. Although Sampras had to save two break points in the third game, there were only another ten points against the serve in that entire set. It was not until the ninth game of the third set that, out of the blue, Sampras – initially putting himself in difficulties with a double fault – was finally broken to love.

From then on, a match that had lived up to the prediction from Sampras's coach, Tim Gullikson, of a 'heavyweight slug-fest' turned decisively in favour of the Croatian. The American's broad shoulders slumped as he was broken in both the first and seventh game of the fourth set. And on his own service games, Ivanisevic continued to rain down the aces, until the total for the day soared, with two more on the last two points, to a personal best of 36. It brought his total for the event, with the final still to come, to 169.

Ivanisevic, who had called for a corset to support his aching back during the quarter-final against Edberg, dismissed fears that there was any major problem there. 'It's a bit sore, but I don't care, for this is a Wimbledon final. Sore back or broken back, you go in and that's it.'

Outside, the race was now on to try and clear up the backlog in other events. But with the mixed doubles still only at the quarter-final stage and some players involved in more than one event, it was already beginning to look as if The Championships might run over to a third Monday, when Miss Seles and Miss Graf, complete with bouquets, walked out for the final of the ladies' singles spot on time.

The match started at 2.08 pm, but it was not until after three rain delays (two of them in excess of an hour and three-quarters) that at 7.29 pm Miss Graf struck a raucous, stinging ace down the middle to bring her a fourth Wimbledon title in five years.

The actual playing time amounted to only 58 minutes, and to some extent the infuriating interruptions – which were made longer than was perhaps necessary due to dire warnings from the London Weather Centre not to take the covers off too soon – reduced the impact of the match

*Anna Smashnova from Israel on her way into the semi-finals of the junior girls' singles.*

*Goran Ivanisevic (left) maintained relentless pressure on Pete Sampras.*

as a spectacle. At the same time, the magnificent manner in which Miss Graf maintained not only her confident composure, but also her resilience and the control of her strident all-court form, was all the more praiseworthy.

For Miss Seles, the 6–2, 6–1 defeat, ending her run of 41 consecutive match wins in Grand Slam tournaments, was the worst she had suffered since 1989 when, as a 15-year-old, she was thrashed, again by Miss Graf, at Wimbledon. It completely shattered her ambition of completing the International Tennis Federation's Grand Slam by holding all four of the world's major titles at the same time – and even more the belief in many quarters that she might do so in the same calendar year.

Apart from Miss Graf's magnificent form from start to finish – her serve had rarely been more effective and the forehand was just unstoppable – the most notable feature of the match was the absence of grunting from Miss Seles, who was clearly responding to the growing hints that unless she at least reduced the volume, then something more than just a friendly request from the umpire's chair might follow.

'I don't think it should have become such a big issue, but I didn't lose because I wasn't grunting,' Miss Seles insisted, accepting a loss, which was clearly hard to take, in a more sporting manner than some of her most ardent supporters were prepared to emulate.

One can only believe the assurance from Miss Seles that it did not affect her. Without doubt, however, she only occasionally produced those famous ripping passes and double-handed backhands, and looked as subdued as she sounded.

Miss Graf, with the crowd undoubtedly behind her, nearly broke Miss Seles's serve in the second game, but finally did so in the fourth. And once she had fought off two break points in the seventh, the first with a fierce forehand crosscourt winner, she was always in control. She was already 1–0 up in the second set before the first rain break of 46 minutes occurred, after which they then only managed to play another five points before hurrying off again, just two minutes after they had resumed.

Part Three saw Miss Graf relentlessly tighten her command. Miss Seles, increasingly prone to unforced errors, double-faulted to 1–3 and was then 15–30 down in the sixth game – just six points from defeat – when, after a further 11 minutes of play, they had to dodge groundstaff dashing on to pull over the court covers, as the rain forced them off yet again.

Just when it seemed as if there was no hope of the match being finished that evening – there was still drizzle in the air and the light was barely acceptable – Miss Graf was summoned from the nearby house in which she was living during the fortnight for one more attempt.

The German, who had dropped only one point thus far in the set on her own serve, made a rare forehand mistake on the first point as Miss Seles fought to keep the match alive, but two more uncharacteristic groundstroke errors made it a lost cause for her. The final game typified, in many ways, the whole match. It began with a reminder of those screaming – though this time they were silent – backhand crosscourt service returns but, as earlier, Miss Graf never allowed her to home in on enough of them. Three forehand winners from Miss Graf followed, the last as she pierced her opponent's backhand corner for the umpteenth time. All that was needed then was the ace on match point.

With the gleaming trophy safely back in her arms after the presentation by HRH The Duchess of Kent, Miss Graf set off on a beaming lap of honour. 'It feels great to win in this way,' she said and, on the absence of the Seles grunt, 'I didn't even notice. I was too focused on what I wanted to do. It's definitely the best I've played for a long time.' Then, after a tribute to her coach, Heinz Guenthardt, she added, 'It was largely a matter of belief. I went out there knowing I had the strokes and there's no doubt the surface suits me better than her. It's a great

satisfaction to beat the number one player in the world in the way I did.'

Meanwhile, on damp courts and in fading light, other matches were still in play for another hour or so until it simply became too dark. Among those delayed were McEnroe and Stich, who had just managed to take the first set on a tie-break from Guy Forget and Jakob Hlasek; and Britain's Miles MacLagan, who earlier in the day had become the first British player since Tony Lloyd (brother of David and John) in 1974 to reach the semi-finals of the boys' singles.

Before lunch, while the sun was still shining, the finalists in the ladies' doubles were settled, when Jana Novotna and Larisa Savchenko-Neiland beat Martina Navratilova and Pam Shriver 7–5, 6–7, 6–3, so ending the latter's hopes that they might equal the record of Suzanne Lenglen and Elizabeth Ryan in winning the title six times. With Gigi Fernandez and Natalia Zvereva beating Arantxa Sanchez Vicario and Helena Sukova, 6–1, 6–7, 7–5, it meant that the final would feature the same four players as in 1991 – but in different formations.

# 13

## Sunday 5 July

# 14

## Monday 6 July

André Agassi's late conversion, like a prodigal son, to the magical mystique – and significance – of Wimbledon, became gloriously complete when, at the end of a marvellous final, tears ran down his cheeks as he stood, not just holding but hugging the trophy to his chest.

The fashion-conscious street urchin from Las Vegas who, for so long, could not understand why so much attention was paid to this annual lawn tennis pilgrimage to a little corner of south-west London, was no longer in any doubt. Indeed, as he savoured the thrill and the reward for 2 hours 50 minutes of quickfire brilliance, which had beaten Goran Ivanisevic 6–7, 6–4, 6–4, 1–6, 6–4, his only regret was that after one year of torture as a teenager, in 1987, he then stayed away until 1991.

'It's sad. This tournament has given my life so much, and it's a shame I didn't respect it earlier,' he said. 'This is the greatest title in the world and this is my greatest achievement.'

The impact of Agassi's triumph spread way beyond compensating a highly talented athlete, whose belief had been in danger of being destroyed by losses in three earlier Grand Slam tournament finals; way beyond justifying the faith of his coach, Nick Bollettieri, who had lived through some dark days with Agassi and had also had his own abilities questioned.

As John Curry, Chairman of The All England Club, said at The Champions' Dinner, 'It's good for the game that someone without the biggest serve in the world can win on grass.'

Behind that glitzy exterior (so much the vogue of the early 1990s) Agassi – blessed with great quickness of eye and feet – had painstakingly developed a style that was also absolutely right for this technological age, a style whereby he could take on the biggest serves and beat them simply by having more broadly based power in his own game.

Not even Goran Ivanisevic, who had pounded Agassi's much-vaunted fellow American, Pete Sampras, into submission 24 hours earlier, could prevent a player who had built his reputation on technicolour shirts and cycle shorts (as much as on his tennis) from deservedly donning the champion's cloak of gold.

Going into the final, Ivanisevic had struck 169 aces, including a personal best of 36 against Sampras. He bettered that by one against Agassi, taking his tally for seven matches during the fortnight to a record 206. Yet just as his powerful serving had been the key to winning the first and fourth sets, so it was his Achilles' heel when the pressure mounted in the fifth.

If ever Agassi was going to crack, as he had done twice at the French Open and once at the US Open (where he

*Previous page: Revenge is sweet for Gigi Fernandez in the final of the ladies' doubles.*

*Goran Ivanisevic (right) was regularly pounded by the speed and ferocity of (overleaf) André Agassi's whiplash forehands.*

never really got started), it would have been at 30–40 in the crucial seventh game of the deciding set. This time it was different. He produced a champion-class serve of his own, then picked the right moment during the rally to steal into the net and put away possibly the most important volley he has played in his life.

To some extent, he had already allowed Ivanisevic back into the match by losing his grip in the fourth set, after spells of totally uninhibited brilliance in the third, when the crown sat back in amazement at the sheer pace, power and audacity of Agassi's returns. Yet three games after Agassi defiantly escaped that break through an opportunity that he had denied Ivanisevic, it was the Croatian who faltered. Serving to stay in the match for the first time, the 6ft 4in left-hander – who had produced at least one ace in all but four of his previous service games, and once (to make it 2–2 in the fifth) as many as four – not only started with his sixth double fault but, to gasps of disbelief from the crowd, repeated the mistake to make it 0–30.

Ivanisevic was desperately close on the next point to yet another double fault, when his second serve only just clipped the corner formed by the centre and service lines. Although he drew level at 30–30, with another service winner, and immediately requested the same ball back to try and repeat the effort, Agassi made a stretching return and followed it with a forehand pass off his opponent's mis-timed half volley, to reach match point.

Again Ivanisevic, in the moment of most need, missed his first serve. Indeed, it landed only a few inches from the bottom of the net, betraying all the tension. Almost in desperation, he came in behind his second serve, but was off-balance and steered a backhand volley against the tape. Agassi fell to the ground and then spreadeagled himself as if in supplication. His shattered opponent stood for a moment, eyes glazed, before stepping over the net and going to congratulate the new champion with 'Listen, man, you deserve it. You played great all these two weeks.'

He admitted that in the end the quality and ferocity of Agassi's returns had been too much for him. 'All the tournament I've been playing guys coming in, and suddenly he stays back. It was different – and it was not easy.' The pattern of Ivanisevic aces – 11 in the first set, seven in the second and five in the third, before another flurry while Agassi was taking a breather in the fourth – told its own story.

Although they were only the eighth and 12th seeds, the lowest combination seen in the final since seeding began, such standings become irrelevant once the quarter-final hurdles have been cleared. And Ivanisevic and Agassi produced a final that was as compulsive and

entertaining as the whole fortnight.

The unconventional American had not only become the first pedigree baseliner since Bjorn Borg to become champion, but the first to do so wearing a hat since the late Yvon Petra in 1946. Although there were a few tut-tuts when the hat stayed in place while he was being presented with the trophy by the President of The All England Club, HRH The Duke of Kent, and while he was being greeted by The Duchess, the cap was absent when Agassi arrived at The Savoy, wearing a black dinner jacket and accompanied by his girlfriend, to be toasted alongside Steffi Graf.

'So do I look better in white or black?' he asked with a wry smile when he began his speech, and went on to say, 'I'm honoured to have this title. I'm not sure if I can live up to it – but I'll try. If my career was to end tomorrow, I've had a lot more than I could ever have asked for.'

Agassi had arrived promptly for The Champions' Dinner at just about the time that extraordinary scenes were still taking place on Court 1, where an epic doubles final between John McEnroe and Michael Stich against Jim Grabb and Richey Reneberg was being halted by officials at 9.22 pm, with the fifth set locked at 13–13. McEnroe and Stich, who wanted what was already the longest doubles final, in terms of games and time, to finish that night, suggested that a tie-break could be the solution. The two Americans were not keen, and it was eventually agreed that everyone would have to return the next morning, when the mixed doubles final and several rounds of the junior doubles still had to be decided.

The two Wimbledon champions, unseeded as a pair, had not lost a set on their way to the final, but they were then stretched almost to breaking point, especially in the final set when, at 6–7, they had to save two match points on Stich's serve. The final had been under way for four and a half hours, if you included the three minutes of heated discussions before the players reluctantly left the court, and, would you believe it, some spectators immediately started the queue for free admission the next day.

It had been a hectic day for all concerned, especially for McEnroe. Before the final and after a doubles semi-final victory over Guy Forget and Jakob Hlasek, which began on Centre Court but was then evicted because of the rain to Court 2 – so as not to delay the men's singles final longer than was absolutely necessary – he was to be found doing his stint in the NBC Television commentary box reporting on the Agassi v Ivanisevic match.

Earlier in the day, Gigi Fernandez and Natalia Zvereva, who had both found themselves abandoned by their respective partners (Jana Novotna and Larisa Savchenko-Neiland) after the 1991 Championships, took sweet revenge in a final featuring new combinations

made out of old, with a 6–4, 6–1 victory in 71 minutes.

For Miss Zvereva, the previous year's winner with Miss Savchenko, it followed up her victory with Miss Fernandez at the French Open. 'We really have fun together, more fun than I've had with any other partner. It really meant something to beat Larisa,' said Miss Zvereva, the second ponytailed blonde celebrating victory at Wimbledon this year.

In the boys' singles, Britain's Miles MacLagan eventually lost his unfinished semi-final against the tall, heavy-serving American Brian Dunn who, in turn, then lost to Czechoslovakia's David Skoch, 6–4, 6–3, in the final. In the girls' singles, the title went to Chanda Rubin, the American beaten in the first round of the ladies' singles by Jennifer Capriati. Miss Rubin, who had dropped only one set in reaching the final, beat Belgium's Laurence Courtois 6–2, 7–5.

As for the old-timers (in age only, not in spirit), who had been entertaining themselves as well as the crowds during the second week, Peter Fleming, who had picked up seven Grand Slam tournament titles with McEnroe in earlier times, won the 35 and Over Men's Invitation Doubles with 1972 singles champion, Stan Smith. Dropping only one set in their group, to John Lloyd and Dick Stockton, before the creases were out of their joints, they beat that wily Australian pair, Peter McNamara and Paul McNamee, in the semi-finals and then two more stubborn Australians, Mark Edmondson and Kim Warwick, 6–7, 7–6, 6–4 in the final.

Marty Riessen and Sherwood Stewart outlasted John Newcombe and Tony Roche, 3–6, 6–3, 6–3, in the final of the 45 and Over Men's Invitation Doubles. Meanwhile, in the 35 and Over Ladies' Invitation Doubles, Wendy Turnbull and Virginia Wade took the title with a 3–6, 6–3, 7–5 finals defeat of Rosie Casals and Sharon Walsh, the latter now a coach working for The Lawn Tennis Association in Britain.

And so to Third Monday which, far from quietly bringing the curtain down on the 106th staging of The Championships, became a memorably exuberant and rapturous farewell. The Centre Court was officially closed, even though at one stage there were nearly 100 people dotted in seats around it. No doubt they were reliving memories from the fortnight, before moving across to Court 1, where Cyril Suk, brother of Helena Sukova, and Larisa Savchenko-Neiland beat the Dutch pair, Jacco Eltingh and Mariam Oremans, 7–5, 6–2, in the final of the mixed doubles.

By now most of the estimated 8,000 fans who had been waiting when the gates opened were inside the grounds, and Court 1 was filled to its 7,500 capacity for what they clearly regarded as the main attraction, even though it

*Lorna Woodroffe and Julie Pullin (facing page) kept the British flag flying into the quarter-finals of the girls' doubles before they lost to the eventual champions.*

*Overleaf (reading clockwise from top left):*
*Australians Steven Baldas and Scott Draper, winners of the junior boys' doubles.*

*Natalia Zvereva and Gigi Fernandez, rivals in the 1991 final, shared the triumph this time in the ladies' doubles.*

*Sherwood Stewart and Marty Riessen take their bows as winners of the 45 and Over Men's Invitation Doubles.*

*David Skoch, the first Czechoslovakian winner of the junior boys' singles since Ivan Lendl in 1978.*

*Cyril Suk and Larisa Savchenko-Neiland, delighted to be mixed doubles champions.*

*Michael Stich and John McEnroe provided a marvellous climax to a memorable tournament when a full-house crowd on Court 1 on the third Monday saw them win a record-breaking men's doubles final.*

*Marija Avotins and Lisa McShea from Australia – winners of the junior girls' doubles.*

*Virginia Wade, still as popular as ever with the crowds as she and Wendy Turnbull won the 35 and Over Ladies' Invitation Doubles.*

might have been over in five minutes.

McEnroe and Stich both found it 'just so exciting and motivating' to discover the enormous queues snaking their way to every entrance, when they arrived to continue their doubles final, that they were actually glad that Grabb and Reneberg had rejected their proposal of a tie-break finish.

Ten more games were played over the next 34 minutes before it was clearly the perfect ending, in the view of the crowd, when McEnroe not only delivered a fabulous top-spin lob that broke the stalemate but then served out for victory.

When Reneberg's final return landed in the net, Stich hugged his partner and lifted him high in the air while, all around, there was cheerful and noisy pandemonium. 'It was one of the best receptions I've ever had. It was incredible to come back today and find the stadium totally full. The energy was incredible and really pumped us up,' McEnroe said after completing his lap of honour and briefly offering the trophy to his 4-year-old son, Sean, on the way. 'It would have been big for us just to have played and won in front of a couple of hundred people. The reception and excitement were just unbelievable.'

The final score was 5–7, 7–6, 6–3, 6–7, 19–17, extending the record for a doubles final to 83 games and 5 hours 1 minute. It was also one of those very special occasions that underlined not only the charisma of McEnroe but also the unique appeal of Wimbledon itself.

Meanwhile, the junior doubles went on. It was late in the afternoon when Steven Baldas and Scott Draper from Australia, who had beaten the British pair, Miles MacLagan and Andrew Richardson, in the semi-finals, beat Mahesh Bhupathi and Nitin Kirtane from India, 6–1, 4–6, 9–7. Marija Avotins and Lisa McShea from Australia beat Pam Nelson and Julie Steven from the United States, 2–6, 6–4, 6–3, in the girls' event.

So ended Wimbledon '92 – one of the best. Kitty Godfree would have loved every minute of it. The champion in 1924 and 1926, who had died, aged 96, just 72 hours before The Championships began, was obviously missed; but, as Steffi Graf so touchingly made clear at The Champions' Dinner, she was far from forgotten.

*Agassi proudly clutching the trophy that meant so much to him and to his coach, Nick Bollettieri.*

*Overleaf: The champions at The Savoy for The Champions' Dinner.*

# CHAMPIONSHIP
# RECORDS 1992

# LIST OF COMPETITORS

Bold figures denote position in Singles Draw

## LADIES

**105** Adams, Miss K. M. *(USA)*
**25** Allen, Miss L. K. *(USA)*
**4** Appelmans, Miss S. *(Belgium)*
- Arendt, Miss N. J. *(USA)*
**3** Babel, Miss M. *(Germany)*
- Bakkum, Miss C. *(Netherlands)*
**42** Basuki, Miss Y. *(Indonesia)*
**102** Baudone, Miss N. *(Italy)*
- Benjamin, Miss C. *(USA)*
**31** Bentley, Miss S. L. *(Great Britain)*
**51** Bollegraf, Miss M. M. *(Netherlands)*
**111** Bonsignori, Miss F. *(Italy)*
- Borneo, Miss B. A. *(Great Britain)*
**5** Bowes, Miss B. A. *(USA)*
**67** Brioukhovets, Miss E. *(CIS)*
- Burgin, Miss E. M. *(USA)*
**2** Byrne, Miss J. M. *(Australia)*
**65** Capriati, Miss J. *(USA)*
- Charles, Miss L. J. *(Great Britain)*
- Collins, Miss S. L. *(USA)*
**120** Cunningham, Miss C. E. *(USA)*
**29** Dahlman, Miss N. *(Finland)*
**98** Daniels, Mrs. P. F. *(USA)*
**16** Date, Miss K. *(Japan)*
**121** de Swardt, Miss M. *(South Africa)*
**60** Dechaume, Miss A. *(France)*
**93** Demongeot, Miss I. *(France)*
**83** Devries, Miss A. *(Belgium)*
- Driehuis, Miss I. *(Netherlands)*
**110** Durie, Miss J. M. *(Great Britain)*
**56** Endo, Miss M. *(Japan)*
**13** Faber, Miss D. L. *(USA)*
**108** Fairbank-Nideffer, Mrs. R. D. *(South Africa)*
**106** Farina, Miss S. *(Italy)*
**95** Fauche, Miss C. *(Switzerland)*
**57** Faull, Miss J.-A. *(Australia)*
**117** Fendick, Miss P. A. *(USA)*
**14** Fernandez, Miss G. *(USA)*
**32** Fernandez, Miss M. J. *(USA)*
**47** Ferrando, Miss L. *(Italy)*
**74** Field, Miss L. *(Australia)*
**37** Frankl, Miss S. *(Germany)*
**27** Frazier, Miss A. *(USA)*
- Fuchs, Miss J. *(USA)*
**55** Fulco-Villella, Mrs. B. *(Argentina)*
**112** Garrison, Miss Z. L. *(USA)*
**122** Garrone, Miss L. *(Italy)*
**6** Gildemeister, Mrs. L. *(Peru)*
- Glitz, Miss L. A. *(USA)*
**88** Godridge, Miss K. *(Australia)*
**28** Golarsa, Miss L. *(Italy)*
**26** Gomer, Miss S. L. *(Great Britain)*
**128** Graf, Miss S. *(Germany)*
**119** Graham, Miss D. A. *(USA)*
- Gregory, Miss L. J. *(South Africa)*
**53** Grunfeld, Miss A. L. *(Great Britain)*
- Guse, Miss K.-A. *(Australia)*
**118** Habsudova, Miss K. *(Czechoslovakia)*
**43** Hack, Miss S. *(Germany)*
**62** Halard, Miss J. *(France)*
**50** Hall, Miss C. *(Great Britain)*
- Harper, Mrs. T. A. *(USA)*
**109** Harvey-Wild, Miss L. M. *(USA)*
**7** Helgeson, Miss G. *(USA)*
**99** Herreman, Miss N. *(France)*
- Hetherington, Miss J. M. *(Canada)*
**89** Hiraki, Miss R. *(Japan)*
- Hodder, Miss J. *(Australia)*
**48** Huber, Miss A. *(Germany)*
**78** Humphreys-Davies, Miss V. S. *(Great Britain)*
**70** Hy, Miss P. *(Canada)*
- Iida, Miss E. *(Japan)*
- Jaggard-Lai, Mrs. M. *(Australia)*
**125** Javer, Miss M. *(Great Britain)*
- Jones, Miss D. J. *(Australia)*
**124** Keller, Miss A. A. *(USA)*
**79** Kidowaki, Miss M. *(Japan)*
- Kijimuta, Miss A. *(Japan)*
**85** Kohde-Kilsch, Miss C. *(Germany)*
**123** Kroupova, Miss K. *(Czechoslovakia)*
**90** Kschwendt, Miss K. *(Germany)*
**15** Kuhlman, Miss C. E. *(USA)*
**41** Labat, Miss F. *(Argentina)*
**12** Lake, Miss V. *(Great Britain)*
- Langrova, Miss P. *(Czechoslovakia)*
**8** Li, Miss F. *(China)*
**116** Lindqvist, Miss C. *(Sweden)*
- Lindstrom, Miss M. *(Sweden)*
**59** Loosemore, Miss S. J. *(Great Britain)*
- Ludloff, Miss H. A. *(USA)*
- MacGregor, Miss C. *(USA)*
- Magers, Mrs. S. W. *(USA)*
**49** Maleeva, Miss K. *(Bulgaria)*
**34** Maleeva, Miss M. *(Bulgaria)*
**81** Maleeva-Fragniere, Mrs. M. *(Switzerland)*
**30** Maniokova, Miss E. *(CIS)*
**107** Martinek, Miss V. *(Germany)*
**97** Martinez, Miss C. *(Spain)*
- McCarthy, Miss S. *(USA)*
**104** McNeil, Miss L. M. *(USA)*
**86** McQuillan, Miss R. *(Australia)*
**20** Medvedeva, Miss N. *(Ukraine)*
**54** Meier, Miss S. *(Germany)*
**63** Meskhi, Miss L. *(Georgia)*
**114** Monami, Miss D. *(Belgium)*
- Morton, Miss T. J. *(Australia)*
**82** Muns-Jagerman, Mrs. N. A. M. *(Netherlands)*
- Nagelsen, Miss B. *(USA)*
**33** Navratilova, Miss M. *(USA)*
**91** Niox-Chateau, Miss S. *(France)*
- Nohakova, Miss A. *(Czechoslovakia)*
- Novelo, Miss L. *(Mexico)*
**113** Novotna, Miss J. *(Czechoslovakia)*
**77** Nowak, Miss K. *(Poland)*
**24** Oeljeklaus, Miss K. *(Germany)*
**87** Oremans, Miss M. *(Netherlands)*
**44** Paradis-Mangon, Mrs. P. *(France)*
- Pfaff, Miss E. S. *(Germany)*
**35** Po, Miss K. *(USA)*
**10** Porwik, Miss C. *(Germany)*
- Pospisilova, Miss J. *(Czechoslovakia)*
- Price, Miss T. A. *(South Africa)*
**22** Probst, Miss W. *(Germany)*
**21** Provis, Miss N. *(Australia)*
- Radford, Miss K. *(Australia)*
**61** Rajchrtova, Miss R. *(Czechoslovakia)*
**69** Reinach, Miss E. *(South Africa)*
- Richardson, Miss J. A. *(New Zealand)*
**84** Rinaldi, Miss K. S. *(USA)*
**39** Rittner, Miss B. *(Germany)*
**66** Rubin, Miss C. *(USA)*
**96** Sabatini, Miss G. *(Argentina)*
- Salmon, Miss J. A. *(Great Britain)*
**64** Sanchez Vicario, Miss A. *(Spain)*
**71** Santrock, Miss J. J. *(USA)*
**9** Savchenko-Neiland, Mrs. L. *(Latvia)*
**76** Sawamatsu, Miss N. *(Japan)*
**18** Schultz, Miss B. *(Netherlands)*
- Segura, Miss A. *(Spain)*
**1** Seles, Miss M. *(Yugoslavia)*
- Sharpe, Miss K. *(Australia)*
**68** Shriver, Miss P. H. *(USA)*
**11** Siddall, Miss S.-A. *(Great Britain)*
**36** Simpson-Alter, Mrs. B. D. *(Canada)*
- Smoller, Miss J. B. *(USA)*
- Smylie, Mrs. P. D. *(Australia)*
- Souto, Miss J. *(Spain)*
- Stafford, Miss S. C. *(USA)*
Strandlund, Miss M. *(Sweden)*
**73** Strnadova, Miss A. *(Czechoslovakia)*
**101** Stubbs, Miss R. P. *(Australia)*
**103** Suire, Miss C. *(France)*
**58** Sukova, Miss H. *(Czechoslovakia)*
**38** Sviglerova, Miss E. *(Czechoslovakia)*
**75** Tanvier, Miss C. *(France)*
**115** Tarabini, Miss P. *(Argentina)*
**17** Tauziat, Miss N. *(France)*
**46** Tessi, Miss C. *(Argentina)*
**45** Testud, Miss S. *(France)*
**72** Thoren, Miss P. *(Finland)*
**127** Van Lottum, Miss N. *(France)*
- Vis, Miss C. M. *(Netherlands)*
**52** Wegink, Miss C. *(Netherlands)*
**126** Werdel, Miss M. *(USA)*
**94** White, Miss R. M. *(USA)*
**40** Whitlinger, Miss T. S. *(USA)*
**92** Whittington, Miss T. *(USA)*
**80** Wiesner, Mrs. H. *(Austria)*
**19** Wood, Miss C. J. *(Great Britain)*
**23** Zrubakova, Miss R. *(Czechoslovakia)*
**100** Zvereva, Miss N. *(CIS)*

## GENTLEMEN

- Acioly, R. *(Brazil)*
- Adams, D. *(Australia)*
**49** Agassi, A. *(USA)*
- Aldrich, P. *(South Africa)*
- Annacone, P. *(USA)*
**23** Azar, R. *(Argentina)*
**20** Bailey, C. B. *(Great Britain)*
**31** Bates, M. J. *(Great Britain)*
- Bathman, R. *(Sweden)*
- Bauer, M. *(USA)*
**33** Becker, B. *(Germany)*
- Beckman, C. *(USA)*
- Bergh, R. *(Sweden)*
**63** Bergstrom, C. *(Sweden)*
**4** Black, B. *(Zimbabwe)*
**75** Boetsch, A. *(France)*
- Borwick, N. *(Australia)*
**70** Braasch, K. *(Germany)*
- Briggs, M. *(USA)*
- Broad, N. *(Great Britain)*
- Brown, J. *(USA)*
- Brown, N. *(Great Britain)*
- Bryan, S. *(USA)*
**34** Camporese, O. *(Italy)*
- Cannon, S. *(USA)*
**56** Carbonell, T. *(Spain)*
- Casal, S. *(Spain)*
**9** Cash, P. *(Australia)*
**26** Castle, A. N. *(Great Britain)*
**28** Champion, T. *(France)*
**32** Chang, M. *(USA)*
**66** Cherkasov, A. *(CIS)*
**50** Chesnokov, A. *(CIS)*
**15** Clavet, F. *(Spain)*
- Connell, G. *(Canada)*
**41** Connors, J. S. *(USA)*
**90** Costa, C. *(Spain)*
**1** Courier, J. *(USA)*
**37** Curren, K. *(USA)*
**35** Damm, M. *(Czechoslovakia)*
- Davids, H. J. *(Netherlands)*
**72** Davis, S. E. *(USA)*
**79** De Jager, J.-L. *(South Africa)*
**13** De la Pena, H. *(Argentina)*
**40** Delaitre, O. *(France)*
- Devries, S. *(USA)*
**120** Doyle, G. *(Australia)*
- Dyke, B. *(Australia)*
- Dzelde, G. *(Latvia)*
**128** Edberg, S. *(Sweden)*
- Eisenman, D. *(USA)*
**10** Eltingh, J. *(Netherlands)*
**48** Ferreira, W. *(South Africa)*
**47** Fitzgerald, J. B. *(Australia)*
- Flach, K. *(USA)*
- Flegl, V. *(Czechoslovakia)*
**82** Fleurian, J. *(France)*
**3** Fontang, F. *(France)*
**17** Forget, G. *(France)*
**116** Foster, A. L. *(Great Britain)*
**91** Frana, J. *(Argentina)*
**84** Fromberg, R. *(Australia)*
- Galbraith, P. *(USA)*
- Garnett, B. *(USA)*
**81** Gilbert, B. *(USA)*
**22** Gilbert, R. *(France)*
**54** Gorriz, M. *(Spain)*
**76** Grabb, J. *(USA)*
- Guenthardt, H. P. *(Switzerland)*
**78** Haarhuis, P. *(Netherlands)*
**42** Herrera, L. E. *(Mexico)*
**61** Hlasek, J. *(Switzerland)*
**119** Holm, H. *(Sweden)*
- Ison, D. P. *(Great Britain)*
**97** Ivanisevic, G. *(Croatia)*
**19** Jarryd, A. *(Sweden)*
- Jensen, L. B. *(USA)*
- Joelson, B. *(USA)*
- Jones, K. *(USA)*
**86** Jonsson, L. *(Sweden)*
- Jonsson, O. *(Sweden)*
**21** Karbacher, B. *(Germany)*
- Keil, M. *(USA)*
- Kempers, T. *(Netherlands)*
**6** Kinnear, K. *(USA)*
**88** Knowles, M. *(Bahamas)*
**87** Koevermans, M. *(Netherlands)*
**64** Korda, P. *(Czechoslovakia)*
**98** Koslowski, L. *(Germany)*
**80** Krajicek, R. *(Netherlands)*
- Kratzmann, M. *(Australia)*
- Kronemann, T. *(USA)*
**52** Kroon, N. *(Sweden)*
- Kruger, S. *(South Africa)*
**111** Kuhnen, P. *(Germany)*
**118** Kulti, N. *(Sweden)*
**92** Larsson, M. *(Sweden)*
**25** Lavalle, L. *(Mexico)*
- Layendecker, G. *(USA)*
**39** Leach, R. *(USA)*
**24** Leconte, H. *(France)*
**112** Lendl, I. *(Czechoslovakia)*
**89** Limberger, C. A. *(Australia)*
**117** Lopez, G. *(Spain)*
- Lundgren, P. *(Sweden)*
- MacLagan, M. *(Great Britain)*
- MacPherson, D. *(Australia)*
**94** Mansdorf, A. *(Israel)*
**60** Markus, G. *(Argentina)*
**14** Martin, T. *(USA)*
**51** Masso, E. *(Belgium)*
**85** Masur, W. *(Australia)*
**44** Matsuoka, S. *(Japan)*
**11** Mattar, L. *(Brazil)*
**12** McEnroe, J. P. *(USA)*
**122** McEnroe, P. *(USA)*
**71** Mezzadri, C. *(Switzerland)*
- Michibata, G. *(Canada)*
**74** Miniussi, C. *(Argentina)*
**121** Montana, F. *(USA)*
**18** Mronz, A. *(Germany)*
**125** Muller, G. *(South Africa)*
**123** Muster, T. *(Austria)*
**93** Naewie, M. *(Germany)*
**69** Nargiso, D. *(Italy)*
- Nelson, T. *(USA)*
- Nijssen, T. *(Netherlands)*
- Norval, P. *(South Africa)*
**106** Novacek, K. *(Czechoslovakia)*
- Nyborg, P. *(Sweden)*
- Odizor, N. *(Nigeria)*
**7** Olhovskiy, A. *(CIS)*
**126** Ondruska, M. *(South Africa)*
- Oosting, M. *(Netherlands)*
- Palmer, J. *(USA)*
- Pate, D. *(USA)*
- Pearce, B. *(USA)*
- Perez, D. *(Uruguay)*
**95** Pescosolido, S. *(Italy)*
**103** Petchey, M. R. J. *(Great Britain)*
- Pimek, L. *(Belgium)*
**57** Pioline, C. *(France)*
**58** Pistolesi, C. *(Italy)*
- Poliakov, D. *(CIS)*
**108** Pozzi, G. *(Italy)*
**36** Pridham, C. *(Canada)*
- Pugh, J. *(USA)*
- Rahnasto, O. *(Finland)*
**104** Randall, D. *(USA)*
**30** Raoux, G. *(France)*
**27** Reneberg, R. A. *(USA)*
**101** Richardson, A. L. *(Great Britain)*
- Rikl, D. *(Czechoslovakia)*
**68** Roese, F. *(Brazil)*
**73** Roig, F. *(Spain)*
**102** Rosset, M. *(Switzerland)*
**55** Rostagno, D. *(USA)*
**59** Saceanu, C. *(Germany)*
- Salumaa, S. *(USA)*
**65** Sampras, P. *(USA)*
**114** Sanchez, E. *(Spain)*
**29** Sanchez, J. *(Spain)*
- Sapsford, D. E. *(Great Britain)*
**62** Schapers, M. *(Netherlands)*
- Scherman, T. *(USA)*
- Seguso, R. *(USA)*
**38** Shelton, B. *(USA)*
**100** Siemerink, J. *(Netherlands)*
**124** Stafford, G. *(South Africa)*
**115** Stankovic, B. *(Czechoslovakia)*
**8** Stark, J. *(USA)*
**5** Steeb, C.-U. *(Germany)*
**96** Stich, M. *(Germany)*
**105** Stolle, S. *(Australia)*
**77** Stoltenberg, J. *(Australia)*
- Suk, C. *(Czechoslovakia)*
- Svantesson, T. *(Sweden)*
- Talbot, B. *(South Africa)*
**46** Tarango, J. *(USA)*
**110** Thoms, A. *(Germany)*
- Thorne, K. *(USA)*
- Vacek, D. *(Czechoslovakia)*
- Van Emburgh, G. *(USA)*
**45** Van Rensburg, C. J. *(South Africa)*
- Visser, D. T. *(South Africa)*
**113** Volkov, A. *(CIS)*
- Warder, L. *(Australia)*
**43** Washington, M. *(USA)*
- Wekesa, P. *(Kenya)*
**16** Wheaton, D. *(USA)*
**107** Wilkinson, C. *(Great Britain)*
**109** Witsken, T. *(USA)*
**67** Woodbridge, T. A. *(Australia)*
**99** Woodforde, M. *(Australia)*
**83** Youl, S. *(Australia)*
**53** Yzaga, J. *(Peru)*
**2** Zoecke, M. *(Germany)*

# EVENT I.—THE GENTLEMEN'S SINGLES CHAMPIONSHIP

**Holder: M. STICH**

The Winner will become the holder, for the year only, of the CHALLENGE CUP presented to the Club by KING GEORGE V, and also of the CHALLENGE CUP presented by The All England Lawn Tennis and Croquet Club. The Winner will receive silver replicas of the two Challenge Cups. A Silver Salver will be presented to the Runner-up and a Bronze Medal to each defeated Semi-finalist.

| FIRST ROUND | SECOND ROUND | THIRD ROUND | FOURTH ROUND | QUARTER-FINALS | SEMI-FINALS | FINAL |
|---|---|---|---|---|---|---|

**FIRST ROUND**

1. J. Courier ① (USA)
2. M. Zoecke (GER)
3. F. Fontang (FRA)
4. B. Black (ZIM)
5. C.-U. Steeb (GER)
6. (Q) K. Kinnear (USA)
7. (Q) A. Olhovskiy (CIS)
8. (Q) J. Stark (USA)
9. (W) P. Cash (AUS)
10. J. Eltingh (NED)
11. L. Mattar (BRA)
12. J. P. McEnroe (USA)
13. H. De la Pena (ARG)
14. T. Martin (USA)
15. F. Clavet (ESP)
16. D. Wheaton ⑯ (USA)
17. G. Forget ⑨ (FRA)
18. A. Mronz (GER)
19. A. Jarryd (SWE)
20. (W) C. B. Bailey (GBR)
21. B. Karbacher (GER)
22. R. Gilbert (FRA)
23. R. Azar (ARG)
24. (W) H. Leconte (FRA)
25. L. Lavalle (MEX)
26. (W) A. N. Castle (GBR)
27. R. A. Reneberg (USA)
28. T. Champion (FRA)
29. J. Sanchez (ESP)
30. (Q) G. Raoux (FRA)
31. M. J. Bates (GBR)
32. M. Chang ⑦ (USA)
33. B. Becker ④ (GER)
34. O. Camporese (ITA)
35. M. Damm (TCH)
36. C. Pridham (CAN)
37. K. Curren (USA)
38. B. Shelton (USA)
39. (Q) R. Leach (USA)
40. O. Delaitre (FRA)
41. J. S. Connors (USA)
42. L. E. Herrera (MEX)
43. M. Washington (USA)
44. S. Matsuoka (JPN)
45. C. J. Van Rensburg (RSA)
46. J. Tarango (USA)
47. (Q) J. B. Fitzgerald (AUS)
48. W. Ferreira ⑭ (RSA)
49. A. Agassi ⑫ (USA)
50. A. Chesnokov (CIS)
51. E. Masso (BEL)
52. (Q) N. Kroon (SWE)
53. J. Yzaga (PER)
54. M. Gorriz (ESP)
55. D. Rostagno (USA)
56. T. Carbonell (ESP)
57. C. Pioline (FRA)
58. C. Pistolesi (ITA)
59. (Q) C. Saceanu (GER)
60. G. Markus (ARG)
61. J. Hlasek (SUI)
62. M. Schapers (NED)
63. C. Bergstrom (SWE)
64. P. Korda ⑥ (TCH)
65. P. Sampras ⑤ (USA)
66. A. Cherkasov (CIS)
67. T. A. Woodbridge (AUS)
68. (L) R. Roese (BRA)
69. D. Nargiso (ITA)
70. K. Braasch (GER)
71. C. Mezzadri (SUI)
72. (Q) S. E. Davis (USA)
73. F. Roig (ESP)
74. C. Miniussi (ARG)
75. A. Boetsch (FRA)
76. J. Grabb (USA)
77. J. Stoltenberg (AUS)
78. P. Haarhuis (NED)
79. J-L. De Jager (RSA)
80. R. Krajicek ⑪ (NED)
81. B. Gilbert ⑬ (USA)
82. J. P. Fleurian (FRA)
83. S. Youl (AUS)
84. R. Fromberg (AUS)
85. W. Masur (AUS)
86. L. Jonsson (SWE)
87. M. Koevermans (NED)
88. (Q) M. Knowles (BAH)
89. (L) C. A. Limberger (AUS)
90. C. Costa (ESP)
91. J. Frana (ARG)
92. M. Larsson (SWE)
93. M. Naewie (GER)
94. A. Mansdorf (ISR)
95. S. Pescosolido (ITA)
96. M. Stich ③ (GER)
97. G. Ivanisevic ⑧ (CRO)
98. L. Koslowski (GER)
99. M. Woodforde (AUS)
100. J. Siemerink (NED)
101. (W) A. L. Richardson (GBR)
102. M. Rosset (SUI)
103. (W) M. R. J. Petchey (GBR)
104. (Q) D. Randall (USA)
105. S. Stolle (AUS)
106. K. Novacek (TCH)
107. (W) C. Wilkinson (GBR)
108. G. Pozzi (ITA)
109. T. Witsken (USA)
110. A. Thoms (GER)
111. P. Kuhnen (GER)
112. I. Lendl ⑩ (TCH)
113. A. Volkov ⑮ (CIS)
114. E. Sanchez (ESP)
115. (Q) B. Stankovic (TCH)
116. (W) A. L. Foster (GBR)
117. G. Lopez (ESP)
118. N. Kulti (SWE)
119. (Q) H. Holm (SWE)
120. (Q) G. Doyle (AUS)
121. F. Montana (USA)
122. P. McEnroe (USA)
123. T. Muster (AUT)
124. (L) G. Stafford (RSA)
125. G. Muller (RSA)
126. (L) M. Ondruska (RSA)
127. (Q) S. Bryan (USA)
128. S. Edberg ② (SWE)

**SECOND ROUND**

- J. Courier ① 6–2, 6–2, 6–3
- B. Black 6–2, 7–5, 6–1
- K. Kinnear 7–6(8–6), 6–2, 6–7(7–9), 6–1
- A. Olhovskiy 6–4, 3–6, 6–3, 3–6, 7–5
- P. Cash 6–4, 6–4, 7–6(7–3)
- J. P. McEnroe 6–7(3–7), 6–4, 5–7, 6–1, 6–3, 6–3
- T. Martin 6–1, 6–0, 6–3
- D. Wheaton ⑯ 6–3, 6–3, 6–3
- G. Forget ⑨ 6–3, 3–6, 7–5, 7–6(7–5)
- A. Jarryd 6–4, 6–3, 6–0
- B. Karbacher 2–6, 7–5, 2–6, 6–4, 6–4
- H. Leconte 6–0, 6–3
- L. Lavalle 6–4, 6–0, 7–6(7–4)
- T. Champion 5–7, 6–4, 3–6, 7–6(7–3), 6–3
- J. Sanchez 6–4, 7–6(7–3), 5–7, 3–6, 9–7
- M. J. Bates 6–4, 6–3, 6–3
- B. Becker ④ 7–5, 6–3, 7–5
- M. Damm 6–4, 6–4, 6–4
- B. Shelton 3–6, 7–6(7–5), 4–6, 7–6(7–5), 9–7
- O. Delaitre 6–1, 7–6(7–4), 3–6, 3–6, 6–3
- L. E. Herrera 6–2, 1–6, 7–5, 6–3
- S. Matsuoka 7–5, 6–4, 6–1
- C. J. Van Rensburg 7–6(7–5), 6–4, 7–5
- W. Ferreira ⑭ 6–2, 6–2, 6–7(2–7), 7–5
- A. Agassi ⑫ 5–7, 6–1, 7–5, 7–5
- E. Masso 6–7(5–7), 6–4, 6–2, 2–6, 6–4
- J. Yzaga 6–4, 6–4, 6–2
- D. Rostagno 2–6, 1–6, 6–1, 6–2
- C. Pioline 6–3, 3–6, 6–3, 7–5
- C. Saceanu 7–5, 6–3, 2–6, 7–5
- J. Hlasek 6–4, 6–3, 6–2
- P. Korda ⑥ 7–5, 7–6(7–4), 6–4
- P. Sampras ⑤ 6–1, 6–3, 6–3
- T. A. Woodbridge 6–2, 7–5, 6–4
- K. Braasch 6–3, 3–6, 6–7(5–7), 7–5, 6–4
- S. E. Davis 6–1, 6–3, 6–3
- F. Roig 6–2, 6–3, 6–4
- A. Boetsch 7–6(7–5), 7–5, 6–4
- P. Haarhuis 6–3, 7–5, 4–6, 4–6, 7–5
- R. Krajicek ⑪ 7–5, 6–1, 6–2
- B. Gilbert ⑬ 6–2, 6–3, 6–2
- S. Youl 6–2, 6–3, 0–1 Ret'd
- W. Masur 6–2, 6–2, 6–1
- M. Knowles 6–2, 6–1, 6–3
- C. Costa 6–1, 4–6, 5–7, 6–3, 6–3
- M. Larsson 6–3, 7–6(7–3), 6–4
- A. Mansdorf 6–3, 7–6(7–4), 6–4
- M. Stich ③ 6–3, 6–3, 6–2
- G. Ivanisevic ⑧ 6–2, 6–2, 6–3
- M. Woodforde 6–2, 6–3, 6–7, 5–7
- M. Rosset 6–2, 6–4, 6–4
- M. R. J. Petchey 7–6(7–1), 6–2, 6–7(5–7), 6–3
- S. Stolle 7–5, 7–6(12–10) Ret'd
- C. Wilkinson 6–3, 6–3, 2–6, 7–6(7–4)
- A. Thoms 6–2, 2–6, 6–2, 6–2
- I. Lendl ⑩ 6–1, 7–6(8–6), 7–6(7–5)
- A. Volkov ⑮ 6–3, 6–2, 4–6, 6–4, 6–3
- B. Stankovic 6–2, 6–4, 6–3
- H. Holm 6–0, 6–0, 6–1
- P. McEnroe 6–3, 6–2, 2–6, 6–4
- G. Stafford 6–4, 6–1, 6–1
- G. Muller 6–3, 6–3, 7–6(8–6)
- S. Edberg ② 6–7(4–7), 6–3, 7–6(10–8), 6–3

**THIRD ROUND**

- J. Courier ① 6–4, 6–1, 6–4
- A. Olhovskiy 6–4, 7–6(7–1), 6–3
- J. P. McEnroe 6–7(3–7), 6–4, 6–7(1–7), 6–3, 6–2
- D. Wheaton ⑯ 6–3, 6–3, 6–7(3–7), 6–3
- G. Forget ⑨ 4–6, 6–3, 3–6, 6–3, 10–8
- H. Leconte 7–5, 6–2, 7–6(7–2)
- T. Champion 7–6(7–5), 6–3, 5–7, 7–5
- M. J. Bates 7–6(7–4), 6–3, 6–4
- B. Becker ④ 4–6, 6–4, 6–4, 3–6, 6–4
- B. Shelton 7–6(7–5), 6–3, 6–3
- L. E. Herrera 6–4, 6–4, 5–7, 4–6, 6–3
- W. Ferreira ⑭ 6–3, 6–3, 6–7(3–7), 6–3
- A. Agassi ⑫ 4–6, 6–1, 6–3, 6–3
- D. Rostagno 6–3, 6–3, 6–1
- C. Saceanu 4–6, 6–4, 0–6, 7–5, 7–5
- J. Hlasek 4–6, 3–6, 6–3, 7–6(9–7), 16–14
- P. Sampras ⑤ 7–6(7–2), 7–6(7–4), 6–7(7–9), 6–4
- S. E. Davis 6–7(5–7), 7–6(7–5), 7–6(7–3), 6–3
- A. Boetsch 6–4, 6–2, 6–2
- R. Krajicek ⑪ 7–6(8–6), 6–3, 6–1
- B. Gilbert ⑬ 6–1, 7–5, 7–6
- W. Masur 6–3, 6–4, 7–6(7–3)
- M. Larsson 7–5, 6–3, 6–7(5–7), 6–4
- M. Stich ③ 6–3, 6–1, 6–3
- G. Ivanisevic ⑧ 6–4, 6–4, 7–6(4–7), 6–3
- M. Rosset 7–6(7–5), 6–2, 6–3
- S. Stolle 3–6, 6–4, 7–6(15–13), 6–4
- I. Lendl ⑩ 7–5, 7–6(8–6), 1–6, 7–5
- A. Volkov ⑮ 6–4, 7–5, 6–3
- H. Holm 6–1, 6–2, 6–2
- G. Stafford 6–4, 7–6(7–3), 2–6, 6–2
- S. Edberg ② 7–6(7–3), 6–3, 7–6(7–4)

**FOURTH ROUND**

- A. Olhovskiy 6–4, 4–6, 6–4, 6–4
- J. P. McEnroe 6–3, 6–4, 6–4
- G. Forget ⑨ 7–6(7–4), 6–3, 3–6, 6–3
- M. J. Bates 7–5, 6–4, 6–7(3–7), 4–6, 6–4
- B. Becker ④ 6–4, 3–6, 7–6(7–5), 7–6(7–5)
- W. Ferreira ⑭ 7–6(7–4), 6–1, 4–6, 6–0
- A. Agassi ⑫ 6–3, 7–6(7–5), 7–5
- C. Saceanu 7–6(7–3), 3–6, 6–3, 1–6, 6–3
- P. Sampras ⑤ 6–1, 6–0, 6–2
- A. Boetsch 4–6, 7–6(8–6), 3–6, 7–6(7–5), 6–2
- W. Masur 6–3, 6–7(2–7), 6–7(5–7), 6–4, 6–2
- M. Stich ③ 7–6(7–4), 6–3, 6–3
- G. Ivanisevic ⑧ 7–6(7–4), 6–4, 6–4
- I. Lendl ⑩ 6–3, 1–6, 2–6, 6–3, 7–5
- H. Holm 6–4, 3–6, 6–3, 7–6(10–8)
- S. Edberg ② 6–1, 6–0, 6–2

**QUARTER-FINALS**

- J. P. McEnroe 7–5, 6–3, 7–6(12–10)
- G. Forget ⑨ 6–7(10–12), 6–4, 3–6, 7–6(7–2), 6–3
- B. Becker ④ 3–6, 6–3, 6–4, 6–7(6–8), 6–1
- A. Agassi ⑫ 7–6(7–1), 6–1, 7–6(7–0)
- P. Sampras ⑤ 6–3, 7–5, 7–6(11–9)
- M. Stich ③ 3–6, 6–1, 6–4, 6–4
- G. Ivanisevic ⑧ 6–7(7–9), 6–1, 6–4, 1–0 Ret'd
- S. Edberg ② 6–3, 6–4, 6–7(1–7), 6–3

**SEMI-FINALS**

- J. P. McEnroe 6–2, 7–6(11–9), 6–3
- A. Agassi ⑫ 4–6, 6–2, 6–2, 4–6, 6–3
- P. Sampras ⑤ 6–3, 6–2, 6–4
- G. Ivanisevic ⑧ 6–7(10–12), 7–5, 6–1, 3–6, 6–3

**FINAL**

- A. Agassi ⑫ 6–4, 6–2, 6–3
- G. Ivanisevic ⑧ 6–7(4–7), 7–6(7–5), 6–4, 6–2

**A. Agassi ⑫ 6–7(8–10), 6–4, 6–4, 1–6, 6–4**

Heavy type denotes seeded players. The encircled figure against names denotes the order in which they have been seeded. (W) = Wild card. (Q) = Qualifier. (L) = Lucky loser.

# EVENT II.—THE GENTLEMEN'S DOUBLES CHAMPIONSHIP     Holders: J. B. FITZGERALD and A. JARRYD

The Winners will become the holders, for the year only, of the CHALLENGE CUPS, presented by the OXFORD UNIVERSITY LAWN TENNIS CLUB and the late SIR HERBERT WILBERFORCE respectively. The Winners will receive silver replicas of the Challenge Cups. A Silver Salver will be presented to each of the Runners-up, and a Bronze Medal to each defeated Semi-finalist.

### FIRST ROUND

```
  1  J. B. Fitzgerald and A. Jarryd ①
  2  P. Aldrich and D. T. Visser
  3  T. Carbonell and D. Rikl
  4  J. P. McEnroe and M. Stich
  5  V. Flegl and K. Novacek
  6  G. Pozzi and O. Rahnasto
(W) 7  C. B. Bailey and C. Wilkinson
  8  K. Kinnear and S. Salumaa ⑮
  9  W. Ferreira and P. Norval ⑩
 10  D. Nargiso and M. Rosset
(W)11  A. N. Castle and C. M. MacLagan
 12  P. Haarhuis and M. Koevermans
(Q)13  H. Holm and P. Nyborg
(Q)14  M. Bauer and B. Joelson
 15  H. J. Davids and L. Pimek
 16  K. Flach and T. Witsken ⑧
 17  K. Jones and R. Leach ③
 18  T. Nelson and J. Stoltenberg
 19  P. Galbraith and J. Palmer
 20  P. Annacone and R. Seguso
(W)21  M. J. Bates and C. J. Van Rensburg
 22  M. Damm and S. Stolle
 23  R. Acioly and B. Black
 24  G. Forget and J. Hlasek ⑬
 25  S. Devries and D. MacPherson ⑪
 26  G. Dzelde and P. Wekesa
(W)27  N. Brown and A. L. Richardson
 28  M. Briggs and T. Kronemann
 29  M. Keil and D. Randall
(Q)30  A. Boetsch and G. Raoux
 31  S. Casal and B. Gilbert
 32  S. E. Davis and D. Pate ⑤
 33  G. Connell and G. Michibata ⑥
 34  C. Beckman and J. Brown
 35  P. McEnroe and J. Stark
 36  B. Dyke and P. Lundgren
 37  N. Odizor and D. Perez
 38  R. Bathman and R. Bergh
 39  B. Pearce and B. Talbot
 40  L. B. Jensen and L. Warder ⑫
 41  J. Frana and L. Lavalle ⑭
 42  D. Adams and A. Olhovskiy
 43  M. Schapers and D. Vacek
(W)44  D. P. Ison and M. R. J. Petchey
 45  P. Korda and J. Pugh
(Q)46  J.-L. De Jager and M. Ondruska
 47  D. Poliakov and J. Siemerink
 48  J. Grabb and R. A. Reneberg ④
 49  T. Nijssen and C. Suk ⑦
 50  K. Curren and G. Muller
 51  J. Eltingh and T. Kempers
 52  B. Garnett and T. Svantesson
 53  S. Kruger and G. Layendecker
 54  C. A. Limberger and M. Oosting
(W)55  A. L. Foster and D. E. Sapsford
 56  M. Kratzmann and W. Masur ⑨
 57  O. Camporese and G. Ivanisevic ⑯
(Q)58  D. Eisenman and M. Knowles
 59  N. Borwick and S. Youl
 60  O. Jonsson and T. Scherman
 61  S. Cannon and G. Van Emburgh
 62  N. Broad and B. Shelton
 63  F. Montana and K. Thorne
 64  T. A. Woodbridge and M. Woodforde ②
```

### SECOND ROUND

```
J. B. Fitzgerald and A. Jarryd ①  6-3, 7-6(7-4), 6-3
J. P. McEnroe and M. Stich  6-2, 6-2, 6-3
G. Pozzi and O. Rahnasto  6-4, 6-3, 6-3
K. Kinnear and S. Salumaa ⑮  6-2, 3-6, 6-3, 7-5
D. Nargiso and M. Rosset  6-3, 6-7(6-8), 4-6, 6-3, 6-4
P. Haarhuis and M. Koevermans  6-4, 6-4, 7-6(7-4)
H. Holm and P. Nyborg  1-6, 6-3, 6-4, 7-6(7-4)
K. Flach and T. Witsken ⑧  7-5, 3-6, 7-6(7-4), 7-6(8-6)
K. Jones and R. Leach ③  6-4, 7-6(7-3), 7-5
P. Galbraith and J. Palmer  3-6, 6-4, 7-6(7-2), 7-6(7-5)
M. J. Bates and C. J. Van Rensburg  6-3, 6-3, 3-6, 7-5
G. Forget and J. Hlasek ⑬  6-3, 7-6(7-2), 6-3
S. Devries and D. MacPherson ⑪  4-6, 7-6(7-2), 7-6(7-5), 3-6, 6-0
N. Brown and A. L. Richardson  6-4, 6-7(5-7), 6-4, 6-3
A. Boetsch and G. Raoux  6-2, 3-6, 6-1, 6-3
S. E. Davis and D. Pate ⑤  6-3, 6-7(5-7), 5-3, Ret d
G. Connell and G. Michibata ⑥  7-5, 6-1, 6-4
P. McEnroe and J. Stark  6-2, 6-3, 6-4
R. Bathman and R. Bergh  7-5, 6-3, 6-2
L. B. Jensen and L. Warder ⑫  6-4, 7-6(7-3), 6-3
J. Frana and L. Lavalle ⑭  6-3, 7-5, 5-7, 3-6, 6-4
M. Schapers and D. Vacek  7-6(9-7), 7-6(7-3), 6-3
J.-L. De Jager and M. Ondruska  2-6, 6-3, 6-3, 6-4, 10-8
J. Grabb and R. A. Reneberg ④  6-3, 6-2, 6-1
K. Curren and G. Muller  7-5, 6-7(3-7), 7-6(7-0), 6-3
J. Eltingh and T. Kempers  4-6, 3-6, 6-4, 7-6(7-5), 6-4
S. Kruger and G. Layendecker  7-5, 6-7(0-7), 3-6, 6-4, 6-3
M. Kratzmann and W. Masur ⑨  6-2, 3-6, 6-4, 6-1
D. Eisenman and M. Knowles  7-6(7-4), 6-7(3-7), 7-6(7-5), 6-2
N. Borwick and S. Youl  6-1, 6-4, 7-6(7-3)
N. Broad and B. Shelton  7-6(7-5), 6-1, 6-3, 7-6(7-3)
T. A. Woodbridge and M. Woodforde ②  1-6, 6-2, 6-2, 6-2
```

### THIRD ROUND

```
J. P. McEnroe and M. Stich  6-3, 7-6(7-3), 6-3
K. Kinnear and S. Salumaa ⑮  6-2, 7-6(8-6), 7-5
P. Haarhuis and M. Koevermans  6-7(5-7), 6-4, 7-6(7-3), 7-5
K. Flach and T. Witsken ⑧  6-2, 6-7(5-7), 7-5
K. Jones and R. Leach ③  3-6, 7-6(7-3), 6-4, 6-3
G. Forget and J. Hlasek ⑬  7-6(7-5), 6-4
S. Devries and D. MacPherson ⑪  6-1, 7-6(7-3), 7-6(9-7)
S. E. Davis and D. Pate ⑤  6-1, 6-2
P. McEnroe and J. Stark  6-4, 7-5, 7-6(7-3)
L. B. Jensen and L. Warder ⑫  3-6, 4-6, 6-1, 6-4, 10-8
J. Frana and L. Lavalle ⑭  7-6(7-4), 6-3, 6-3, 7-5
J. Grabb and R. A. Reneberg ④  6-2, 7-5, 6-4
J. Eltingh and T. Kempers  6-3, 4-6, 7-6(7-4), 7-6(7-5)
M. Kratzmann and W. Masur ⑨  6-4, 6-4, 6-4
N. Borwick and S. Youl  7-6(7-2), 6-3, 6-3
T. A. Woodbridge and M. Woodforde ②  6-3, 7-6(8-6), 7-6(8-6)
```

### QUARTER-FINALS

```
J. P. McEnroe and M. Stich  6-3, 6-2, 6-4
P. Haarhuis and M. Koevermans  6-4, 6-4, 6-2
G. Forget and J. Hlasek ⑬  6-3, 6-4, 6-4
S. E. Davis and D. Pate ⑤  6-3, 6-7(3-7), 6-3, 6-4
P. McEnroe and J. Stark  6-2, 6-4, 4-6, 6-4
J. Grabb and R. A. Reneberg ④  6-1, 6-2, 6-4
M. Kratzmann and W. Masur ⑨  6-7(3-7), 6-4, 6-3, 3-6, 8-6
T. A. Woodbridge and M. Woodforde ②  6-7(3-7), 6-4, 6-3
```

### SEMI-FINALS

```
J. P. McEnroe and M. Stich  6-3, 6-4, 6-4
G. Forget and J. Hlasek ⑬  4-6, 7-6(8-6), 6-7(2-7), 6-4
J. Grabb and R. A. Reneberg ④  6-7(5-7), 6-3, 7-5, 6-3
T. A. Woodbridge and M. Woodforde ②
```

### FINAL

```
J. P. McEnroe and M. Stich  7-6(7-4), 6-3, 7-6(7-4)
J. Grabb and R. A. Reneberg ④  7-6(7-5), 4-6, 7-6(7-4), 6-4
```

### CHAMPIONS

```
J. P. McEnroe and M. Stich  5-7, 7-6(7-5), 3-6, 7-6(7-5), 19-17
```

Heavy type denotes seeded players. The encircled figure against names denotes the order in which they have been seeded. (W) – Wild card. (Q) – Qualifier. (L) – Lucky loser. The Matches will be the best of five sets.

## EVENT III.—THE LADIES' SINGLES CHAMPIONSHIP

The Winner will become the holder, for the year only, of the CHALLENGE TROPHY presented by The All England Lawn Tennis and Croquet Club. The Winner will receive a silver replica of the Trophy. A Silver Salver will be presented to the Runner-up and a Bronze Medal to each defeated Semi-finalist.

### FIRST ROUND

|  |  |  |
|---|---|---|
| 1 | **Miss M. Seles** ① | (YUG) |
| 2 | Miss J. M. Byrne | (AUS) |
| 3 | Miss M. Babel | (GER) |
| 4 | Miss S. Appelmans | (BEL) |
| 5 | Mrs. B. A. Bowes | (USA) |
| 6 | Miss L. Gildemeister | (PER) |
| 7 | Miss G. Helgeson | (USA) |
| 8 | Miss F. Li | (CHN) |
| 9 | Mrs. L. Savchenko-Neiland | (LAT) |
| 10 | Miss C. Porwik | (GER) |
| (W) 11 | Miss S-A. Siddall | (GBR) |
| (W) 12 | Miss V. Lake | (GBR) |
| 13 | Miss D. L. Faber | (USA) |
| 14 | Miss G. Fernandez | (USA) |
| 15 | Miss C. E. Kuhlman | (USA) |
| 16 | **Miss K. Date** ⑤ | (JPN) |
| 17 | **Miss N. Tauziat** ④ | (FRA) |
| 18 | Miss B. Schultz | (NED) |
| (W) 19 | Miss C. J. Wood | (GBR) |
| 20 | Miss N. Medvedeva | (UKR) |
| 21 | Miss N. Provis | (AUS) |
| 22 | Miss W. Probst | (GER) |
| 23 | Miss R. Zrubakova | (TCH) |
| 24 | Miss K. Oeljeklaus | (GER) |
| 25 | Miss L. K. Allen | (USA) |
| 26 | Miss S. L. Gomer | (GBR) |
| 27 | Miss A. Frazier | (USA) |
| 28 | Miss L. Golarsa | (ITA) |
| 29 | Miss N. Dahlman | (FIN) |
| 30 | Miss E. Maniokova | (CIS) |
| (W) 31 | Miss S. L. Bentley | (GBR) |
| 32 | **Miss M. J. Fernandez** ⑦ | (USA) |
| 33 | **Miss M. Navratilova** ④ | (USA) |
| 34 | Miss M. Maleeva | (BUL) |
| 35 | Miss K. Po | (USA) |
| 36 | Mrs. B. D. Simpson-Alter | (CAN) |
| 37 | Miss S. Frankl | (GER) |
| 38 | Miss E. Sviglerova | (TCH) |
| 39 | Miss B. Rittner | (GER) |
| 40 | Miss T. S. Whitinger | (USA) |
| 41 | Miss F. Labat | (ARG) |
| 42 | Miss Y. Basuki | (INA) |
| 43 | Miss S. Hack | (GER) |
| 44 | Miss P. Paradis-Mangon | (FRA) |
| 45 | Miss S. Testud | (FRA) |
| (Q) 46 | Miss C. Tessi | (ARG) |
| 47 | Miss L. Ferrando | (ITA) |
| 48 | **Miss A. Huber** ⑩ | (GER) |
| 49 | **Miss K. Maleeva** ⑫ | (BUL) |
| (W) 50 | Miss C. Hall | (GBR) |
| 51 | Miss M. M. Bollegraf | (NED) |
| (Q) 52 | Miss C. Wegink | (NED) |
| (W) 53 | Miss A. L. Grunfeld | (GBR) |
| 54 | Miss S. Meier | (GER) |
| 55 | Miss B. Fulco-Villella | (ARG) |
| 56 | Miss M. Endo | (JPN) |
| (L) 57 | Miss J.-A. Faull | (AUS) |
| 58 | Miss H. Sukova | (TCH) |
| (W) 59 | Miss S. J. Loosemore | (GBR) |
| 60 | Miss A. Dechaume | (FRA) |
| 61 | Miss R. Rajchrtova | (TCH) |
| 62 | Miss J. Halard | (FRA) |
| 63 | Miss L. Meskhi | (GEO) |
| 64 | **Miss A. Sanchez Vicario** ⑤ | (ESP) |
| 65 | **Miss J. Capriati** ⑥ | (USA) |
| 66 | Miss C. Rubin | (USA) |
| 67 | Miss E. Brioukhovets | (CIS) |
| 68 | Miss P. H. Shriver | (USA) |
| 69 | Miss E. Reinach | (RSA) |
| 70 | Miss P. Hy | (CAN) |
| (Q) 71 | Miss J. J. Santrock | (USA) |
| 72 | Miss P. Thoren | (FIN) |
| 73 | Miss A. Strnadova | (TCH) |
| (Q) 74 | Miss L. Field | (AUS) |
| 75 | Miss C. Tanvier | (FRA) |
| 76 | Miss N. Sawamatsu | (JPN) |
| 77 | Miss K. Nowak | (POL) |
| (W) 78 | Miss V. S. Humphreys-Davis | (GBR) |
| 79 | Miss M. Kidowaki | (JPN) |
| 80 | **Mrs. H. Wiesner** ⑯ | (AUT) |
| 81 | **Mrs. M. Maleeva-Fragniere** ⑨ | (SUI) |
| 82 | Mrs. N. A. M. Muns-Jagerman | (NED) |
| (Q) 83 | Miss A. Devries | (BEL) |
| 84 | Miss K. S. Rinaldi | (USA) |
| 85 | Miss C. Kohde-Kilsch | (GER) |
| 86 | Miss R. McQuillan | (AUS) |
| (Q) 87 | Miss M. Oremans | (NED) |
| 88 | Miss K. Godridge | (AUS) |
| (Q) 89 | Miss R. Hiraki | (JPN) |
| (Q) 90 | Miss K. Kschwendt | (GER) |
| 91 | Miss S. Niox-Chateau | (FRA) |
| (L) 92 | Miss T. Whittington | (USA) |
| 93 | Miss R. M. White | (USA) |
| 94 | Miss I. Demongeot | (FRA) |
| 95 | Miss C. Fauche | (SUI) |
| 96 | **Miss G. Sabatini** ③ | (ARG) |
| 97 | **Miss C. Martinez** ⑧ | (ESP) |
| 98 | Mrs. P. F. Daniels | (USA) |
| 99 | Miss N. Herreman | (FRA) |
| 100 | Miss N. Zvereva | (CIS) |
| 101 | Miss R. P. Stubbs | (AUS) |
| 102 | Miss N. Baudone | (ITA) |
| 103 | Miss C. Suire | (FRA) |
| 104 | Miss L. M. McNeil | (USA) |
| 105 | Miss K. M. Adams | (USA) |
| 106 | Miss S. Farina | (ITA) |
| 107 | Miss V. Martinek | (GER) |
| 108 | Mrs. R. D. Fairbank-Nideffer | (RSA) |
| 109 | Miss L. M. Harvey-Wild | (USA) |
| 110 | Miss J. M. Durie | (GBR) |
| 111 | Miss F. Bonsignori | (ITA) |
| 112 | **Miss Z. L. Garrison** ⑬ | (USA) |
| 113 | **Miss J. Novotna** ⑪ | (TCH) |
| 114 | Miss D. Monami | (BEL) |
| 115 | Miss P. Tarabini | (ARG) |
| 116 | Miss C. Lindqvist | (SWE) |
| 117 | Miss P. A. Fendick | (USA) |
| 118 | Miss K. Habsudova | (TCH) |
| 119 | Miss D. A. Graham | (USA) |
| 120 | Miss C. E. Cunningham | (USA) |
| 121 | Miss M. de Swardt | (RSA) |
| 122 | Miss L. Garrone | (ITA) |
| 123 | Miss K. Kroupova | (TCH) |
| 124 | Miss A. A. Keller | (USA) |
| 125 | Miss M. Javer | (GBR) |
| 126 | Miss M. Werdel | (USA) |
| 127 | Miss N. Van Lottum | (FRA) |
| 128 | **Miss S. Graf** ② | (GER) |

### SECOND ROUND

- Miss M. Seles ① — 6-2, 6-2
- Miss S. Appelmans — 6-0, 6-2
- Mrs. L. Gildemeister — 6-0, 6-2
- Miss G. Helgeson — 6-1, 6-2
- Miss C. Porwik — 6-0, 6-3
- Miss S-A. Siddall — 2-6, 6-4, 6-3
- Miss G. Fernandez — 6-4, 4-6, 6-3
- Miss K. Date ⑤ — 7-6(7-2), 6-2
- Miss N. Tauziat ④ — 6-4, 6-0
- Miss N. Medvedeva — 6-3, 6-3
- Miss N. Provis — 6-0, 6-3
- Miss R. Zrubakova — 6-1, 6-1
- Miss L. K. Allen — 3-6, 6-1, 7-5
- Miss A. Frazier — 6-2, 6-1
- Miss N. Dahlman — 7-6(10-8), 6-4
- Miss M. J. Fernandez ⑦ — 6-1, 6-0
- Miss M. Navratilova ④ — 6-2, 6-2
- Miss K. Po — 6-4, 6-3
- Miss S. Frankl — 6-2, 6-0
- Miss B. Rittner — 6-4, 6-1
- Miss Y. Basuki — 6-2, 6-2
- Miss S. Hack — 6-3, 1-6, 12-10
- Miss C. Tessi — 4-6, 6-3, 6-4
- Miss A. Huber ⑩ — 6-4, 6-4
- Miss K. Maleeva ⑫ — 6-2, 6-2
- Miss M. M. Bollegraf — 6-1, 6-2
- Miss A. L. Grunfeld — 4-6, 6-2, 6-4
- Miss M. Endo — 6-1, 6-2
- Miss H. Sukova — 3-6, 6-1, 7-5
- Miss A. Dechaume — 6-1, 4-6, 6-4
- Miss J. Halard — 6-3, 6-1
- Miss A. Sanchez Vicario ⑤ — 6-3, 7-6(7-3)
- Miss J. Capriati ⑥ — 6-0, 7-5
- Miss P. H. Shriver — 1-6, 6-3, 6-1
- Miss P. Hy — 6-4, 6-2
- Miss P. Thoren — 6-3, 7-6(7-5)
- Miss A. Strnadova — 6-2, 6-2
- Miss N. Sawamatsu — 6-2, 7-5
- Miss K. Nowak — 6-3, 6-0
- Mrs. H. Wiesner ⑯ — 6-2, 6-2
- Mrs. M. Maleeva-Fragniere ⑨ — 6-1, 6-4
- Miss K. S. Rinaldi — 6-2, 7-6(7-4)
- Miss C. Kohde-Kilsch — 2-6, 6-2, 6-4
- Miss K. Godridge — 6-3, 6-3
- Miss R. Hiraki — 6-0, 6-3
- Miss T. Whittington — 6-1, 4-6, 7-5
- Miss I. Demongeot — 6-2, 6-3
- Miss G. Sabatini ③ — 6-1, 6-1
- Miss C. Martinez ⑧ — 6-1, 6-0
- Miss N. Zvereva — 6-3, 6-2
- Miss R. P. Stubbs — 6-2, 7-5
- Miss L. M. McNeil — 6-1, 7-5
- Miss K. M. Adams — 6-3, 6-2
- Mrs. R. D. Fairbank-Nideffer — 7-6(7-4), 6-1
- Miss L. M. Harvey-Wild — 6-4, 6-2
- Miss Z. L. Garrison ⑬ — 6-0, 6-1
- Miss J. Novotna ⑪ — 6-1, 6-2
- Miss C. Lindqvist — 6-2, 6-4
- Miss P. A. Fendick — 6-2, 6-4
- Miss D. A. Graham — 6-2, 7-6(7-4)
- Miss M. de Swardt — 6-4, 6-3
- Miss A. A. Keller — 6-3, 6-4
- Miss M. Werdel — 6-2, 4-6, 6-0
- Miss S. Graf ② — 6-1, 6-0

### THIRD ROUND

- Miss M. Seles ① — 6-3, 6-2
- Mrs. L. Gildemeister — 3-6, 6-4, 7-5
- Miss C. Porwik — 6-4, 6-2
- Miss G. Fernandez — 6-1, 6-3
- Miss N. Tauziat ④ — 7-5, 2-6, 6-3
- Miss N. Provis — 6-2, 6-4
- Miss A. Frazier — 7-6(7-3), 6-1
- Miss M. J. Fernandez ⑦ — 7-5, 6-2
- Miss M. Navratilova ④ — 6-2, 3-6, 6-0
- Miss B. Rittner — 6-0, 6-0
- Miss Y. Basuki — 7-5, 6-3
- Miss A. Huber ⑩ — 6-2, 6-2
- Miss K. Maleeva ⑫ — 6-4, 6-1
- Miss M. Endo — 5-7, 6-2, 7-5
- Miss H. Sukova — 7-5, 6-2
- Miss J. Halard — 6-3, 2-6, 6-3
- Miss J. Capriati ⑥ — 6-2, 6-4
- Miss P. Hy — 6-2, 6-7(5-7), 6-1
- Miss N. Sawamatsu — 6-3, 7-6(9-7)
- Mrs. H. Wiesner ⑯ — 6-0, 6-1
- Mrs. M. Maleeva-Fragniere ⑨ — 4-6, 6-3, 6-4
- Miss K. Godridge — 6-4, 7-5
- Miss R. Hiraki — 6-1, 7-5
- Miss G. Sabatini ③ — 6-2, 6-3
- Miss N. Zvereva — 6-3, 5-7, 6-4
- Miss L. M. McNeil — 6-1, 6-3
- Mrs. R. D. Fairbank-Nideffer — 6-3, 6-4
- Miss Z. L. Garrison ⑬ — 6-2, 6-4
- Miss J. Novotna ⑪ — 6-3, 6-2
- Miss P. A. Fendick — 7-5, 7-5
- Miss M. de Swardt — 6-2, 5-7, 7-5
- Miss S. Graf ② — 6-1, 6-1

### FOURTH ROUND

- Miss M. Seles ① — 6-4, 6-1
- Miss G. Fernandez — 6-2, 6-0
- Miss N. Tauziat ④ — 4-6, 7-5, 6-3
- Miss A. Frazier — 6-3, 6-3
- Miss M. Navratilova ④ — 7-5, 6-1
- Miss Y. Basuki — 6-2, 6-3
- Miss K. Maleeva ⑫ — 7-5, 6-3
- Miss J. Halard — 4-6, 6-1, 6-3
- Miss J. Capriati ⑥ — 6-3, 6-1
- Miss N. Sawamatsu — 6-1, 7-5
- Miss K. Godridge — 7-5, 7-6(7-2)
- Miss G. Sabatini ③ — 6-0, 6-4
- Miss N. Zvereva — 5-7, 6-4, 7-5
- Miss Z. L. Garrison ⑬ — 6-4, 6-2
- Miss P. A. Fendick — 6-3, 6-3
- Miss S. Graf ② — 5-7, 6-0, 7-5

### QUARTER-FINALS

- Miss M. Seles ① — 6-4, 6-2
- Miss N. Tauziat ④ — 6-0, 6-3
- Miss M. Navratilova ④ — 7-5, 6-2
- Miss K. Maleeva ⑫ — 6-0, 6-3
- Miss J. Capriati ⑥ — 6-3, 4-6, 6-4
- Miss G. Sabatini ③ — 6-2, 6-1
- Miss N. Zvereva — 6-2, 3-6, 6-1
- Miss S. Graf ② — 4-6, 6-3, 6-2

### SEMI-FINALS

- Miss M. Seles ① — 6-1, 6-3
- Miss M. Navratilova ④ — 6-3, 7-6(7-2)
- Miss G. Sabatini ③ — 6-1, 3-6, 6-4
- Miss S. Graf ② — 6-3, 6-1

### FINAL

- Miss M. Seles ① — 6-2, 6-7(3-7), 6-4
- **Miss S. Graf** ② — 6-3, 6-3

### WINNER

**Miss S. Graf** ② — 6-2, 6-1

---

Heavy type denotes seeded players. The encircled figure against names denotes the order in which they have been seeded. (W) Wild card. (Q) Qualifier. (L) Lucky loser. The Matches will be the best of three sets.

# EVENT IV.—THE LADIES' DOUBLES CHAMPIONSHIP          Holders: Miss L. SAVCHENKO and Miss N. ZVEREVA

The Winners will become the holders, for the year, of the CHALLENGE CUP presented by H.R.H. PRINCESS MARINA, DUCHESS OF KENT, the late President of The All England Lawn Tennis and Croquet Club. The Winners will receive silver replicas of the Challenge Cup. A Silver Salver will be presented to each of the Runners-up and a Bronze Medal to each defeated Semi-finalist.

| | FIRST ROUND | SECOND ROUND | THIRD ROUND | QUARTER-FINALS | SEMI-FINALS | FINAL |
|---|---|---|---|---|---|---|

**FIRST ROUND**

1. Miss J. Novotna and Mrs. L. Savchenko-Neiland ①
2. Miss C. Benjamin and Miss J. J. Santrock
3. Miss K. Date and Miss M. Kidowaki
4. Miss J. Fuchs and Miss K. Habsudova
5. Mrs. B. Fulco-Villella and Miss J. B. Smoller
6. Miss L. Meskhi and Mrs. H. Wiesner
(Q) 7. Miss J. Hodder and Miss K. Sharpe
8. Miss P. A. Fendick and Miss A. Strnadova ⑨
9. Mrs. S. W. Magers and Miss R. M. White ⑯
10. Miss L. Garrone and Miss L. Golarsa
11. Miss S. C. Stafford and Miss M. Werdel
12. Miss Y. Basuki and Miss J. M. Durie
(Q) 13. Miss C. Bakkum and Miss M. Strandlund
14. Miss L. A. Glitz and Miss C. E. Kuhlman
15. Miss A. Frazier and Miss R. Hiraki
16. Miss K. M. Adams and Miss M. M. Bollegraf ⑥
17. Miss M. Navratilova and Miss P. H. Shriver ④
18. Mrs. M. Jaggard-Lai and Miss C. M. Vis
(W) 19. Mrs. R. D. Fairbank-Nideffer and Miss B. Nagelsen
20. Mrs. P. Paradis-Mangon and Miss S. Testud
21. Miss K. Godridge and Miss K. Kschwendt
22. Miss K.-A. Guse and Miss T. J. Morton
23. Miss M. Babel and Miss W. Probst
24. Miss A. Huber and Miss C. Kohde-Kilsch ④
25. Miss R. McQuillan and Miss C. Porwik ⑫
26. Miss J.-A. Faull and Miss J. A. Richardson
(Q) 27. Miss A. Kijimuta and Miss N. Sawamatsu
28. Miss J. M. Byrne and Miss P. Tarabini
29. Miss J. Pospisilova and Miss N. Van Lottum
(W) 30. Miss C. Hall and Miss S.-A. Siddall
31. Miss E. M. Burgin and Miss M. de Swardt
32. Miss J. M. Hetherington and Miss K. S. Rinaldi ⑧
33. Miss M. J. Fernandez and Miss Z. L. Garrison ⑤
34. Miss N. J. Arendt and Miss S. McCarthy
(W) 35. Miss A. L. Grunfeld and Miss J. A. Salmon
36. Miss S. Farina and Miss L. Ferrando
37. Miss E. S. Pfaff and Miss C. Suire
38. Miss L. Field and Miss L. J. Gregory
39. Miss A. Dechaume and Miss J. Halard
40. Miss S. L. Collins and Miss E. Reinach ⑩
41. Miss K. Maleeva and Miss B. Rittner ⑮
42. Miss D. A. Graham and Miss G. Helgeson
43. Mrs. L. Gildemeister and Miss F. Labat
44. Miss A. Segura and Miss J. Souto
45. Miss P. Langrova and Miss R. Zrubakova
46. Miss E. Iida and Miss M. Lindstrom
47. Miss B. A. Borneo and Miss C. J. Wood
48. Miss A. Sanchez Vicario and Miss H. Sukova ③
49. Miss L. M. McNeil and Miss R. P. Stubbs ⑦
50. Mrs. T. A. Harper and Miss C. MacGregor
51. Miss E. Brioukhovets and Miss N. Medvedeva
52. Miss P. F. Daniels and Miss L. M. Harvey-Wild
(Q) 53. Miss D. J. Jones and Miss T. A. Price
(W) 54. Miss M. Javer and Miss V. Lake
55. Miss S. Appelmans and Miss M. Oremans
56. Miss I. Demongeot and Miss N. Tauziat ⑬
57. Miss N. Provis and Mrs. P. D. Smylie ⑪
58. Miss H. A. Ludloff and Miss C. Martinez
59. Miss L. Novelo and Miss K. Radford
60. Miss A. Nohakova and Miss R. Rajchrtova
61. Miss M. Maleeva and Mrs. M. Maleeva-Fragniere
62. Mrs. N. A. M. Muns-Jagerman and Miss B. Schultz
63. Miss B. A. Bowes and Miss T. S. Whitlinger
64. Miss G. Fernandez and Miss N. Zvereva ②

**SECOND ROUND**

- Miss J. Novotna and Mrs. L. Savchenko-Neiland ①  6-4, 6-4
- Miss J. Fuchs and Miss K. Habsudova  7-6(7-5), 6-3
- Miss L. Meskhi and Mrs. H. Wiesner  6-2, 3-1 Ret'd
- Miss P. A. Fendick and Miss A. Strnadova ⑨  6-3, 6-2
- Mrs. S. W. Magers and Miss R. M. White ⑯  7-5, 6-3
- Miss Y. Basuki and Miss J. M. Durie  6-0, 6-1
- Miss C. Bakkum and Miss M. Strandlund  6-3, 6-1
- Miss K. M. Adams and Miss M. M. Bollegraf ⑥  6-1, 6-2
- Miss M. Navratilova and Miss P. H. Shriver ④  6-1, 6-2
- Mrs. R. D. Fairbank-Nideffer and Miss B. Nagelsen  6-3, 6-4
- Miss K.-A. Guse and Miss T. J. Morton  6-7(3-7), 6-3, 6-1
- Miss A. Huber and Miss C. Kohde-Kilsch ④  2-6, 6-3, 6-2
- Miss J.-A. Faull and Miss J. A. Richardson  6-4, 4-6, 6-3
- Miss A. Kijimuta and Miss N. Sawamatsu  6-2, 6-0
- Miss J. Pospisilova and Miss N. Van Lottum  7-6(7-3), 6-3
- Miss E. M. Burgin and Miss M. de Swardt  6-2, 6-3
- Miss M. J. Fernandez and Miss Z. L. Garrison ⑤  6-2, 6-4
- Miss S. Farina and Miss L. Ferrando  3-6, 6-1, 6-1
- Miss L. Field and Miss L. J. Gregory  6-4, 6-4
- Miss S. L. Collins and Miss E. Reinach ⑩  6-4, 7-5
- Miss K. Maleeva and Miss B. Rittner ⑮  4-6, 7-6(7-4), 6-3
- Mrs. L. Gildemeister and Miss F. Labat  7-6(9-7), 6-1
- Miss E. Iida and Miss M. Lindstrom  6-4, 6-3
- Miss A. Sanchez Vicario and Miss H. Sukova ③  6-2, 1-6, 6-2
- Miss L. M. McNeil and Miss R. P. Stubbs ⑦  6-2, 6-4
- Miss E. Brioukhovets and Miss N. Medvedeva  7-6(7-3), 6-2
- Miss D. J. Jones and Miss T. A. Price  3-6, 6-0, 6-1
- Miss I. Demongeot and Miss N. Tauziat ⑬  2-6, 6-4, 7-5
- Miss H. A. Ludloff and Miss C. Martinez  6-4, 4-6, 6-1
- Miss L. Novelo and Miss K. Radford  6-4, 6-4
- Mrs. N. A. M. Muns-Jagerman and Miss B. Schultz  6-7(4-7), 6-2, 7-5
- Miss G. Fernandez and Miss N. Zvereva ②  6-2, 6-1

**THIRD ROUND**

- Miss J. Novotna and Mrs. L. Savchenko-Neiland ①  6-3, 6-1
- Miss P. A. Fendick and Miss A. Strnadova ⑨  6-4, 6-1
- Mrs. S. W. Magers and Miss R. M. White ⑯  6-1, 6-4
- Miss K. M. Adams and Miss M. M. Bollegraf ⑥  4-6, 6-3, 6-0
- Miss M. Navratilova and Miss P. H. Shriver ④  6-4, 6-7(4-7), 7-5
- Miss A. Huber and Miss C. Kohde-Kilsch ④  6-3, 6-7(5-7), 6-2
- Miss J.-A. Faull and Miss J. A. Richardson  6-2, 6-3
- Miss E. M. Burgin and Miss M. de Swardt  7-5, 6-3
- Miss M. J. Fernandez and Miss Z. L. Garrison ⑤  6-2, 6-3
- Miss S. L. Collins and Miss E. Reinach ⑩  6-3, 6-2
- Miss K. Maleeva and Miss B. Rittner ⑮  6-0, 4-6, 7-5
- Miss A. Sanchez Vicario and Miss H. Sukova ③  7-6(7-2), 6-1
- Miss L. M. McNeil and Miss R. P. Stubbs ⑦  7-5, 2-6, 6-4
- Miss I. Demongeot and Miss N. Tauziat ⑬  6-7(7-9), 6-2, 12-10
- Miss L. Novelo and Miss K. Radford  4-6, 6-3, 8-6
- Miss G. Fernandez and Miss N. Zvereva ②  6-3, 6-2

**QUARTER-FINALS**

- Miss J. Novotna and Mrs. L. Savchenko-Neiland ①  6-2, 6-2
- Mrs. S. W. Magers and Miss R. M. White ⑯  6-4, 3-6, 6-2
- Miss M. Navratilova and Miss P. H. Shriver ④  6-1, 6-2
- Miss J.-A. Faull and Miss J. A. Richardson  6-4, 5-7, 6-0
- Miss M. J. Fernandez and Miss Z. L. Garrison ⑤  6-7(5-7), 6-4, 6-2
- Miss A. Sanchez Vicario and Miss H. Sukova ③  6-4, 6-2
- Miss L. M. McNeil and Miss R. P. Stubbs ⑦  6-4, 6-4
- Miss G. Fernandez and Miss N. Zvereva ②  6-2, 6-7(6-8), 6-2

**SEMI-FINALS**

- Miss J. Novotna and Mrs. L. Savchenko-Neiland ①  6-2, 7-6(7-4)
- Miss M. Navratilova and Miss P. H. Shriver ④  6-3, 6-1
- Miss A. Sanchez Vicario and Miss H. Sukova ③  6-2, 6-4
- Miss G. Fernandez and Miss N. Zvereva ②  6-0, 6-3

**FINAL**

- Miss J. Novotna and Mrs. L. Savchenko-Neiland ①  7-5, 6-7(3-7), 6-3
- Miss G. Fernandez and Miss N. Zvereva ②  6-1, 6-7(2-7), 7-5

**Winner:** Miss G. Fernandez and Miss N. Zvereva ②  6-4, 6-1

Heavy type denotes seeded players. The encircled figure against names denotes the order in which they have been seeded. (W) = Wild card. (Q) = Qualifier. (L) = Lucky loser. The Matches will be the best of three sets.

# EVENT V.—THE MIXED DOUBLES CHAMPIONSHIP

**Holders: J. B. FITZGERALD and Mrs. P. D. SMYLIE**

The Winners will become the holders, for the year, of the CHALLENGE CUP presented by the family of the late Mr. S. H. SMITH. The Winners will receive silver replicas of the Challenge Cup. A Silver Salver will be presented to each of the Runners-up and a Bronze Medal to each defeated Semi-finalist.

| FIRST ROUND | SECOND ROUND | THIRD ROUND | QUARTER-FINALS | SEMI-FINALS | FINAL |
|---|---|---|---|---|---|
| 1 T. A. Woodbridge and Miss J. Novotna ① | T. A. Woodbridge and Miss J. Novotna ① 7–6(7–5), 7–6(7–2) | T. A. Woodbridge and Miss J. Novotna ① 6–3, 7–5 | | | |
| 2 B. Talbot and Miss I. Demongeot | | | | | |
| 3 T. Kronemann and Miss G. Helgeson | K. Kinnear and Mrs. R. D. Fairbank-Nideffer 4–6, 7–5, 6–3 | | T. A. Woodbridge and Miss J. Novotna ① 6–2, 7–5 | | |
| 4 K. Kinnear and Mrs. R. D. Fairbank-Nideffer | | | | | |
| 5 B. Black and Miss C. E. Kuhlman | J. Pugh and Miss N. Zvereva 6–4, 6–4 | J. Pugh and Miss N. Zvereva 6–2, 7–6(7–3) | | | |
| 6 J. Pugh and Miss N. Zvereva | | | | | |
| 7 L. Lavalle and Miss L. Novelo | J.B. Fitzgerald and Mrs. P. D. Smylie ⑨ 6–3, 6–1 | | | T. Nijssen and Miss M. M. Bollegraf⑧ 6–3, 0–6, 9–7 | |
| 8 J. B. Fitzgerald and Mrs. P. D. Smylie ⑨ | | | | | |
| 9 G. Connell and Miss K. S. Rinaldi ⑪ | G. Connell and Miss K. S. Rinaldi ⑪ 6–4, 6–0 | M. J. Bates and Miss J. M. Durie 6–3, 7–6(7–5) | | | |
| 10 R. Bathman and Miss C. Suire | | | | | |
| 11 O. Rahnasto and Miss K. Habsudova | M. J. Bates and Miss J. M. Durie 6–2, 6–2 | | T. Nijssen and Miss M. M. Bollegraf ⑧ 6–4, 7–5 | | |
| 12 M. J. Bates and Miss J. M. Durie | | | | | |
| 13 M. Briggs and Mrs. M. Jaggard-Lai | M. Briggs and Mrs. M. Jaggard-Lai 2–6, 6–3, 6–4 | T. Nijssen and Miss M. M. Bollegraf ⑧ 6–4, 6–4 | | | |
| 14 M. Oosting and Mrs. N. A. M. Muns-Jagerman | | | | | |
| 15 N. Borwick and Miss E. Iida | T. Nijssen and Miss M. M. Bollegraf ⑧ 6–4, 6–4 | | | | |
| 16 T. Nijssen and Miss M. M. Bollegraf ⑧ | | | | | |
| 17 R. Leach and Miss Z. L. Garrison ④ | R. Leach and Miss Z. L. Garrison ④ 6–4, 6–2 | J. Stark and Miss D. A. Graham 6–4, 6–7(6–8), 8–6 | | | |
| 18 P. Aldrich and Miss L. J. Gregory | | | | | |
| 19 J. Stark and Miss D. A. Graham | J. Stark and Miss D. A. Graham 6–2, 6–4 | | J. Stark and Miss D. A. Graham 2–6, 7–6(8–6), 6–0 | | |
| (W) 20 M. R. J. Petchey and Miss S. J. Loosemore | | | | | |
| 21 B. Garnett and Miss K. Radford | K. Flach and Miss L. M. Harvey-Wild 6–4, 6–7(8–10), 6–3 | M. Schapers and Miss B. Schultz w/o | | | |
| 22 K. Flach and Miss L. M. Harvey-Wild | | | | | J. Eltingh and Miss M. Oremans 5–7, 7–6(7–3), 6–4 |
| 23 M. Schapers and Miss B. Schultz | M. Schapers and Miss B. Schultz 4–6, 7–6(7–3), 6–4 | | | J. Eltingh and Miss M. Oremans 7–6(7–3), 6–4 | |
| 24 S. Devries and Miss P. A. Fendick ⑭ | | | | | |
| 25 L. Warder and Miss R. P. Stubbs ⑮ | L. Warder and Miss R. P. Stubbs ⑮ 6–4, 3–6, 6–3 | L. Warder and Miss R. P. Stubbs ⑮ 6–3, 6–4 | | | |
| 26 G. Dzelde and Miss L. Meskhi | | | | | |
| 27 P. Norval and Miss M. de Swardt | V. Flegl and Miss R. Zrubakova 3–6, 7–5, 6–2 | | J. Eltingh and Miss M. Oremans 6–3, 6–4 | | |
| 28 V. Flegl and Miss R. Zrubakova | | | | | |
| 29 J. Eltingh and Miss M. Oremans | J. Eltingh and Miss M. Oremans 7–6(7–5), 5–7, 6–4 | J. Eltingh and Miss M. Oremans 3–6, 6–4, 6–4 | | | |
| 30 R. Bergh and Miss S. Appelmans | | | | | |
| 31 S. Salumaa and Miss J.-A. Faull | S. Salumaa and Miss J.-A. Faull 3–6, 7–5, 7–5 | | | | |
| 32 M. Michibata and Miss J. M. Hetherington ⑥ | | | | | |
| 33 M. Woodforde and Miss N. Provis ⑦ | M. Woodforde and Miss N. Provis ⑦ 6–2, 6–2 | M. Woodforde and Miss N. Provis ⑦ 6–2, 6–3 | | | |
| 34 A. Olhovskiy and Miss S. L. Collins | | | | | |
| 35 L. Pimek and Miss P. Langrova | L. Pimek and Miss P. Langrova 3–6, 6–3, 6–4 | | J. Stoltenberg and Miss A. Strnadova 6–2, 7–5 | | |
| (W) 36 C. Wilkinson and Miss S. L. Gomer | | | | | |
| 37 J. Stoltenberg and Miss A. Strnadova | J. Stoltenberg and Miss A. Strnadova 6–4, 6–7(3–7), 6–4 | J. Stoltenberg and Miss A. Strnadova 6–2, 6–4 | | | |
| 38 C. Beckman and Mrs. T. A. Harper | | | | | |
| 39 D. Vacek and Miss C. Porwik | D. Vacek and Miss C. Porwik 6–3, 5–7, 6–2 | | | C. Suk and Mrs. L. Savchenko-Neiland ③ 4–6, 6–4, 8–6 | |
| 40 D. MacPherson and Miss R. McQuillan ⑩ | | | | | |
| 41 T. Witsken and Miss K. M. Adams ⑬ | T. Kempers and Miss C. M. Vis 6–4, 7–6(8–6) | J. Frana and Miss G. Sabatini 7–6(7–5), 7–5 | | | |
| 42 T. Kempers and Miss C. M. Vis | | | | | |
| 43 N. Broad and Miss C. J. Wood | J. Frana and Miss G. Sabatini 6–7(4–7), 7–5, 14–12 | | C. Suk and Mrs. L. Savchenko-Neiland ③ w/o | | |
| (W) 44 J. Frana and Miss G. Sabatini | | | | | |
| 45 B. Dyke and Miss C. MacGregor | B. Dyke and Miss C. MacGregor 6–3, 6–4 | C. Suk and Mrs. L. Savchenko-Neiland ③ 7–5, 6–2 | | | |
| 46 S. Youl and Miss L. Field | | | | | |
| (W) 47 H. P. Guenthardt and Miss S. Graf | C. Suk and Mrs. L. Savchenko-Neiland ③ 6–4, 6–4 | | | | C. Suk and Mrs. L. Savchenko-Neiland③ 7–6(7–2), 6–2 |
| 48 C. Suk and Mrs. L. Savchenko-Neiland ③ | | | | | |
| 49 K. Jones and Miss G. Fernandez ⑤ | K. Jones and Miss G. Fernandez ⑤ 6–1, 4–6, 6–3 | K. Jones and Miss G. Fernandez ⑤ 3–6, 7–5, 9–7 | | | |
| 50 P. Galbraith and Miss T. J. Morton | | | | | |
| 51 D. T. Visser and Miss E. Reinach | D. T. Visser and Miss E. Reinach 6–2, 6–2 | | B. Shelton and Miss L. M. McNeil 6–3, 7–5 | | |
| 52 G. Van Emburgh and Miss S. McCarthy | | | | | |
| 53 B. Shelton and Miss L. M. McNeil | B. Shelton and Miss L. M. McNeil 6–4, 6–2 | B. Shelton and Miss L. M. McNeil 4–6, 7–6(7–5), 11–9 | | | |
| 54 J. Siemerink and Miss I. Driehuis | | | | | |
| 55 D. Adams and Miss K.-A. Guse | M. Kratzmann and Miss P. H. Shriver ⑫ 7–5, 6–3 | | | C. Suk and Mrs. L. Savchenko-Neiland ③ 7–6(7–5), 6–4 | |
| 56 M. Kratzmann and Miss P. H. Shriver ⑫ | | | | | |
| 57 S. E. Davis and Miss R. M. White ⑯ | L. B. Jensen and Miss J. Capriati 6–3, 6–2 | L. B. Jensen and Miss J. Capriati 6–2, 7–6(9–7) | | | |
| 58 L. B. Jensen and Miss J. Capriati | | | | | |
| 59 T. Nelson and Mrs. S. W. Magers | T. Nelson and Mrs. S. W. Magers 5–7, 6–3, 6–4 | | L. B. Jensen and Miss J. Capriati 6–3, 6–3 | | |
| 60 D. Randall and Miss W. Probst | | | | | |
| (W) 61 P. Annacone and Miss E. M. Burgin | M. Keil and Miss N. Van Lottum 6–2, 6–3 | A. Jarryd and Miss H. Sukova ② 6–4, 6–4 | | | |
| 62 M. Keil and Miss N. Van Lottum | | | | | |
| 63 J. Brown and Miss S. C. Stafford | A. Jarryd and Miss H. Sukova ② 6–2, 6–3 | | | | |
| 64 A. Jarryd and Miss H. Sukova ② | | | | | |

Heavy type denotes seeded players. The encircled figure against names denotes the order in which they have been seeded. (W) = Wild card. (Q) = Qualifier. (L) = Lucky loser. The Matches will be the best of three sets.

The Winners will become the holders, for the year only, of a Cup presented by The All England Lawn Tennis and Croquet Club. The Winners will receive miniature Silver Salvers, a Silver Medal will be presented to each of the Runners-up.

## GROUP A

| | | | | WINS | LOSSES |
|---|---|---|---|:---:|:---:|
| **T. E. Gullikson and T. R. Gullikson** | J. G. Alexander and P. C. Dent<br>6–2, 6–2 | C. Dowdeswell and A. J. Stone<br>3–6, 7–5, 6–3 | P. Barthes and B. Taroczy<br>6–1, 6–2 | 3 | 0 |
| J. G. Alexander and P. C. Dent | **T. E. Gullikson and T. R. Gullikson**<br>2–6, 2–6 | P. Barthes and B. Taroczy<br>3–6, 7–6(7–2), 6–4 | C. Dowdeswell and A. J. Stone<br>7–6(7–5), 6–7(5–7), 3–6 | 1 | 2 |
| C. Dowdeswell and A. J. Stone | P. Barthes and B. Taroczy<br>3–6, 6–1, 6–4 | **T. E. Gullikson and T. R. Gullikson**<br>6–3, 5–7, 3–6 | J. G. Alexander and P. C. Dent<br>6–7(5–7), 7–6(7–5), 6–3 | 2 | 1 |
| P. Barthes and B. Taroczy | C. Dowdeswell and A. J. Stone<br>6–3, 1–6, 4–6 | J. G. Alexander and P. C. Dent<br>6–3, 6–7(2–7), 4–6 | **T. E. Gullikson and T. R. Gullikson**<br>1–6, 2–6 | 0 | 3 |

## GROUP B

| | | | | WINS | LOSSES |
|---|---|---|---|:---:|:---:|
| **P. Slozil and T. Smid** | M. R. Edmondson and K. Warwick<br>6–4, 6–3 | P. Dupre and H. Pfister<br>6–7(5–7), 6–7(4–7) | R. Tanner and E. J. van Dillen<br>6–7(6–8), 6–2, 6–4 | 2 | 1 |
| M. R. Edmondson and K. Warwick | **P. Slozil and T. Smid**<br>4–6, 3–6 | R. Tanner and E. J. van Dillen<br>6–2, 6–3 | P. Dupre and H. Pfister<br>7–6(7–3), 7–6(7–4) | 2 | 1 |
| P. Dupre and H. Pfister | R. Tanner and E. J. van Dillen<br>3–6, 2–6 | **P. Slozil and T. Smid**<br>7–6(7–5), 7–6(7–4) | M. R. Edmondson and K. Warwick<br>6–7(3–7), 6–7(4–7) | 1 | 2 |
| R. Tanner and E. J. van Dillen | P. Dupre and H. Pfister<br>6–3, 6–2 | M. R. Edmondson and K. Warwick<br>2–6, 3–6 | **P. Slozil and T. Smid**<br>7–6(8–6), 2–6, 4–6 | 1 | 2 |

## GROUP C

| | | | | WINS | LOSSES |
|---|---|---|---|:---:|:---:|
| **P. Fleming and S. R. Smith** | J. M. Lloyd and R. L. Stockton<br>4–6, 6–4, 6–4 | A. Amritraj and V. Amritraj<br>6–4, 6–4 | R. L. Case and G. Masters<br>7–5, 6–2 | 3 | 0 |
| J. M. Lloyd and R. L. Stockton | **P. Fleming and S. R. Smith**<br>6–4, 4–6, 4–6 | R. L. Case and G. Masters<br>6–1, 6–3 | A. Amritraj and V. Amritraj<br>2–6, 3–6 | 1 | 2 |
| A. Amritraj and V. Amritraj | R. L. Case and G. Masters<br>6–2, 6–7(6–8), 6–1 | **P. Fleming and S. R. Smith**<br>4–6, 4–6 | J. M. Lloyd and R. L. Stockton<br>6–2, 6–3 | 2 | 1 |
| R. L. Case and G. Masters | A. Amritraj and V. Amritraj<br>2–6, 7–6(8–6), 1–6 | J. M. Lloyd and R. L. Stockton<br>1–6, 3–6 | **P. Fleming and S. R. Smith**<br>5–7, 2–6 | 0 | 3 |

## GROUP D

| | | | | WINS | LOSSES |
|---|---|---|---|:---:|:---:|
| **P. B. McNamara and P. F. McNamee** | R. J. Frawley and C. J. Lewis<br>6–4, 3–6, 7–5 | R. C. Lutz and A. A. Mayer<br>6–3, 7–6(7–4) | J. W. Feaver and P. Hutchins<br>6–4, 6–3 | 3 | 0 |
| R. J. Frawley and C. J. Lewis | **P. B. McNamara and P. F. McNamee**<br>4–6, 6–3, 5–7 | J. W. Feaver and P. Hutchins<br>6–2, 7–5 | R. C. Lutz and A. A. Mayer<br>6–7(3–7), 2–6 | 1 | 2 |
| R. C. Lutz and A. A. Mayer | J. W. Feaver and P. Hutchins<br>6–1, 6–2 | **P. B. McNamara and P. F. McNamee**<br>3–6, 6–7(4–7) | R. J. Frawley and C. J. Lewis<br>7–6(7–3), 6–2 | 2 | 1 |
| J. W. Feaver and P. Hutchins | R. C. Lutz and A. A. Mayer<br>1–6, 2–6 | R. J. Frawley and C. J. Lewis<br>2–6, 5–7 | **P. B. McNamara and P. F. McNamee**<br>4–6, 3–6 | 0 | 3 |

**SEMI-FINAL**

T. E. Gullikson and T. R. Gullikson
v
M. R. Edmondson and K. Warwick

P. Fleming and S. R. Smith
v
P. B. McNamara and P. F. McNamee

**FINAL**

M. R. Edmondson and K. Warwick
7–5, 7–6(7–5)

P. Fleming and S. R. Smith
7–5, 6–3

**Winner:** P. Fleming and S. R. Smith 6–7(5–7), 7–6(7–5), 6–4

This event will be played on a 'round robin' basis. 16 invited pairs have been divided into 4 groups and each pair in each group will play one another. The pairs winning most matches will be the winners of their respective groups and will play semi-final and final rounds as indicated above.

If matches should be equal in any group, sets won will be counted and, should these be equal, the percentage of games won to the percentage of games played, will determine the winning pair of a group.

Heavy type denotes seeded players. The encircled figure against names denotes the order in which they have been seeded. The Matches will be the best of three sets.
The tie-break will operate at six games all in the first two sets.

## EVENT VII.—THE 45 AND OVER GENTLEMEN'S INVITATION DOUBLES

The Winners will become the holders, for the year only, of a Cup presented by The All England Lawn Tennis and Croquet Club. The Winners will receive a miniature Silver Salvers, a Silver Medal will be presented to each of the Runners-up.

| | FIRST ROUND | SEMI- FINALS | FINAL | |
|---|---|---|---|---|
| 1 | **M. C. Reissen and S. E. Stewart** ① | **M. C. Reissen and S. E. Stewart** ① 6–1, 6–2 | **M. C. Reissen and S. E. Stewart** ① 6–4, 6–4 | |
| 2 | A. Metreveli and R. Taylor | | | |
| 3 | **K. R. Rosewall and F. S. Stolle** ③ | **K. R. Rosewall and F. S. Stolle** ③ 7–6(7–3), 7–6(7–5) | | |
| 4 | J. Fillol and J. Kodes | | | |
| 5 | J. R. Cooper and N. A. Fraser | **R. A. J. Hewitt and F. D. McMillan** ④ 6–2, 6–4 | | |
| 6 | **R. A. J. Hewitt and F. D. McMillan** ④ | | **J. D. Newcombe and A. D. Roche** ② 6–1, 6–2 | |
| 7 | I. Nastase and T. S. Okker | **J. D. Newcombe and A. D. Roche** ② 6–3, 7–6(7–4) | | |
| 8 | **J. D. Newcombe and A. D. Roche** ② | | | |

**M. C. Reissen and S. E. Stewart** ① 3–6, 6–3, 6–3

Heavy type denotes seeded players. The encircled figure against names denotes the order in which they have been seeded. The Matches will be the best of three sets.
The tie-break will operate at six games all in the first two sets.

## EVENT VIII.—THE 35 AND OVER LADIES' INVITATION DOUBLES   Holders: Miss W.M. TURNBULL and Miss S.V. WADE

The Winners will become the holders, for the year only, of a Cup presented by The All England Lawn Tennis and Croquet Club. The Winners will receive miniature Cups, a Silver Medal will be presented to each of the Runners-up.

| | FIRST ROUND | SEMI-FINALS | FINAL | |
|---|---|---|---|---|
| 1 | **Miss W. M. Turnbull and Miss S. V. Wade** ① | **Miss W. M. Turnbull and Miss S. V. Wade** ① 6–2, 6–1 | **Miss W. M. Turnbull and Miss S. V. Wade** ① 6–3, 6–2 | |
| 2 | Miss M. Michel and Miss Y. Vermaak | | | |
| 3 | **Mrs. W. W. Bowrey and Mrs. D. E. Dalton** ③ | Miss M. Jausovec and Mrs. O. Morozova 6–3, 6–3 | | |
| 4 | Miss M. Jausovec and Mrs. O. Morozova | | | |
| 5 | Miss H. Gourlay and Miss J. C. Russell | **Mrs. F. Durr and Miss B. F. Stove** ④ 2–6, 7–6(7–4), 7–5 | | |
| 6 | **Mrs. F. Durr and Miss B. F. Stove** ④ | | **Miss R. Casals and Miss S. A. Walsh** ② 3–6, 6–2, 6–1 | |
| 7 | Miss L. J. Charles and Mrs. G. E. Reid | **Miss R. Casals and Miss S. A. Walsh** ② 6–3, 6–3 | | |
| 8 | **Miss R. Casals and Miss S. A. Walsh** ② | | | |

**Miss W. M. Turnbull and Miss S. V. Wade** ① 3–6, 6–3, 7–5

Heavy type denotes seeded players. The encircled figure against names denotes the order in which they have been seeded. The Matches will be the best of three sets.
The tie-break will operate at six games all in the first two sets.

# EVENT IX.—THE BOYS' SINGLES CHAMPIONSHIP

**Holder: T. ENQVIST**

The Winner will become the holder, for the year only, of a Cup presented by The All England Lawn Tennis and Croquet Club. The Winner and Runner-up will each receive a personal prize.

| FIRST ROUND | SECOND ROUND | THIRD ROUND | QUARTER-FINALS | SEMI-FINALS | FINAL |
|---|---|---|---|---|---|
| 1  G. Doyle ① (AUS) | G. Doyle ①  6-0, 6-0 | G. Doyle ①  6-3, 6-3 | G. Doyle ①  6-2, 6-2 | | |
| 2  S. Chukhan (THA) | | | | | |
| 3  S. Leiner (AUT) | S. Leiner  6-4, 6-4 | | | | |
| 4  A. Radulescu (—) | | | | | |
| 5  B. A. Cowan (GBR) | B. A. Cowan  6-3, 5-7, 6-4 | B. A. Cowan  7-5, 6-1 | | | |
| 6  G. A. Degreef (ARG) | | | | | |
| 7  P. Joromsky (CIS) | F. Kascak ⑮  6-1, 6-4 | | | D. Skoch ⑩  7-5, 6-3 | |
| 8  F. Kascak ⑮ (TCH) | | | | | |
| 9  D. Skoch ⑩ (TCH) | D. Skoch ⑩  7-5, 6-2 | D. Skoch ⑩  6-4, 0-6, 6-2 | D. Skoch ⑩  6-2, 2-6, 6-2 | | |
| 10  G. Fernandes (BRA) | | | | | |
| 11  E. Abaroa (MEX) | E. Abaroa  6-2, 6-2 | | | | |
| 12  T. H. Henman (GBR) | | | | | |
| 13  V. Spadea (USA) | V. Spadea  6-4, 6-0 | H.-K. Song ⑧  7-6(11-9), 6-2 | | | |
| 14  R. Reddy (IND) | | | | | |
| 15  L. Ilou (CIV) | H.-K. Song ⑧  7-6(7-1), 6-4 | | | | |
| 16  H.-K. Song ⑧ (KOR) | | | | | D. Skoch ⑩  7-5, 5-7, 6-4 |
| 17  A. Pavel ③ (ROM) | A. Pavel ③  5-7, 6-4, 6-4 | A. Pavel ③  3-6, 6-1, 6-4 | A. Pavel ③  7-6(7-3), 6-3 | | |
| 18  P. Braga (BRA) | | | | | |
| 19  B. Jacob (GER) | B. Jacob  6-1, 6-1 | | | | |
| 20  J. Delgado (GBR) | | | | | |
| 21  G. Carraz (FRA) | G. Carraz  6-2, 7-5 | G. Carraz  6-2, 6-4 | | A. Pavel ③  6-3, 6-3 | |
| 22  S. Yongchantanasakul (THA) | | | | | |
| 23  S. Draper (AUS) | S. Draper  6-1, 6-2 | | | | |
| 24  A. Zingman ⑭ (ARG) | | | | | |
| 25  G. Diaz ⑪ (ARG) | S. S. Koehler  6-1, 6-2 | S. S. Koehler  6-2, 6-3 | A. Savolt  6-3, 3-6, 6-3 | | |
| 26  S. S. Koehler (HKG) | | | | | |
| 27  E. Taino (USA) | M. Bhupathi  6-4, 6-3 | | | | |
| 28  M. Bhupathi (IND) | | | | | |
| 29  A. Savolt (HUN) | A. Savolt  4-6, 6-3, 6-1 | A. Savolt  6-4, 6-4 | | | |
| 30  E. Casas (MEX) | | | | | |
| 31  T. Suzuki (JPN) | A. L. Richardson ⑥  6-0, 6-3 | | | | |
| 32  A. L. Richardson ⑥ (GBR) | | | | | D. Skoch ⑩  6-4, 6-3 |
| 33  A. Ferreira ⑤ (BRA) | A. Ferreira ⑤  6-3, 7-6(8-6) | S. Manai  6-4, 6-4 | S. Manai  7-6(7-5), 6-3 | | |
| 34  D. Miketa (TCH) | | | | | |
| 35  S. Manai (SUI) | S. Manai  6-7(4-7), 6-3, 6-2 | | | | |
| 36  G. A. Etlis (ARG) | | | | | |
| 37  S. Downs (NZL) | S. Downs  6-3, 6-4 | S. Downs  7-6(8-6), 6-3 | | B. Dunn ④  6-2, 7-6(7-4) | |
| 38  L. J. Sabin (GBR) | | | | | |
| 39  F. Bergh (SWE) | N. Kirtane ⑫  7-6(11-9), 7-5 | | | | |
| 40  N. Kirtane ⑫ (IND) | | | | | |
| 41  N. Ploysook ⑬ (THA) | T. Harel Ben Simon  7-6(7-2), 6-2 | N. Godwin  7-5, 7-5 | B. Dunn ④  5-7, 7-5, 6-1 | | |
| 42  T. Harel Ben Simon (ISR) | | | | | |
| 43  A. Belobrajdic (AUS) | N. Godwin  6-1, 6-0 | | | | |
| 44  N. Godwin (RSA) | | | | | |
| 45  D. J. Sanders (GBR) | D. J. Sanders  7-6(7-3), 7-6(7-4) | B. Dunn ④  6-3, 6-3 | | | |
| 46  L. Olguin (ARG) | | | | | |
| 47  J. J. Esqueda (MEX) | B. Dunn ④  4-6, 6-1, 8-6 | | | | B. Dunn ④  6-2, 6-4 |
| 48  B. Dunn ④ (USA) | | | | | |
| 49  C. M. MacLagan ⑦ (GBR) | C. M. MacLagan ⑦  6-0, 6-1 | C. M. MacLagan ⑦  6-3, 7-6(7-5) | C. M. MacLagan ⑦  7-5, 6-3 | | |
| 50  M. J. Misa (PHI) | | | | | |
| 51  C. A. Reano (PER) | L. Arnold  6-2, 6-4 | | | | |
| 52  L. Arnold (ARG) | | | | | |
| 53  O. Tauma (FRA) | O. Tauma  6-4, 6-3 | O. Tauma  6-2, 3-6, 6-4 | | C. M. MacLagan ⑦  6-3, 6-0 | |
| 54  V. Reddy (IND) | | | | | |
| 55  J. J. Jackson (USA) | J. J. Jackson  7-6(8-6), 6-3 | | | | |
| 56  N. Behr ⑨ (ISR) | | | | | |
| 57  H. Wiltschnig ⑯ (AUT) | J. Greenhalgh  6-7(2-7), 6-3, 6-2 | S. Baldas  5-7, 6-3, 15-13 | S. Ladipo  6-3, 1-6, 7-5 | | |
| 58  J. Greenhalgh (NZL) | | | | | |
| 59  S. Baldas (AUS) | S. Baldas  6-4, 7-6(7-2) | | | | |
| 60  M. Schofield (GBR) | | | | | |
| 61  S. Ladipo (NGR) | S. Ladipo  7-5, 6-3 | S. Ladipo  6-3, 6-1 | | | |
| 62  S. Adbib (MAR) | | | | | |
| 63  C. Halim (INA) | C. Halim  4-6, 7-6(8-6), 7-5 | | | | |
| 64  G. Silberstein ② (CHI) | | | | | |

Heavy type denotes seeded players. The encircled figure against names denotes the order in which they have been seeded. The Committee reserves the right to alter the seeding order in the event of withdrawals. The Matches will be the best of three sets.

---

# EVENT X.—THE BOYS' DOUBLES CHAMPIONSHIP

**Holders: K. ALAMI and G. RUSEDSKI**

The Winners will become the holders, for the year only, of a Cup presented by The All England Lawn Tennis and Croquet Club. The Winners and Runners-up will each receive a personal prize.

| FIRST ROUND | SECOND ROUND | QUARTER-FINALS | SEMI-FINALS | FINAL |
|---|---|---|---|---|
| 1  C. M. MacLagan and A. L. Richardson ① | C. M. MacLagan and A. L. Richardson ①  4-6, 6-1, 6-0 | C. M. MacLagan and A. L. Richardson ①  6-3, 5-7, 9-7 | | |
| 2  N. Behr and C. Halim | | | | |
| 3  N. Godwin and G. Williams | N. Godwin and G. Williams  6-2, 7-6(7-4) | | C. M. MacLagan and A. L. Richardson ①  5-7, 7-6(7-1), 6-2 | |
| 4  S. Downs and P. Joromsky | | | | |
| 5  J. Jaramillo and B. Saluja | N. Baglin and M. Coombs  6-4, 6-2 | N. Baglin and M. Coombs  7-6(7-2), 7-5) | | |
| 6  N. Baglin and M. Coombs | | | | |
| 7  N. Ploysook and T. Suzuki | N. Ploysook and T. Suzuki  6-3, 6-4 | | | |
| 8  E. Casas and A. Ferreira ⑦ | | | | |
| 9  S. Baldas and S. Draper ③ | S. Baldas and S. Draper ③  6-4, 3-6, 6-0 | S. Baldas and S. Draper ③  6-2, 6-4 | | S. Baldas and S. Draper ③  7-6(7-5), 6-4 |
| 10  S. Leiner and H. Wiltschnig | | | | |
| 11  J. J. Jackson and E. Taino | J. J. Jackson and E. Taino  6-7(5-7), 7-5, 6-3 | | S. Baldas and S. Draper ③  6-1, 6-7(3-7), 6-3 | |
| 12  B. A. Cowan and L. J. Sabin | | | | |
| 13  S. Manai and A. Savolt | L. Arnold and G. A. Etlis  6-4, 6-2 | L. Arnold and G. A. Etlis  6-0, 6-4 | | |
| 14  L. Arnold and G. A. Etlis | | | | |
| 15  M. J. Misa and V. Reddy | F. Kascak and D. Skoch ⑥  6-1, 6-1 | | | |
| 16  F. Kascak and D. Skoch ⑥ | | | | |
| 17  G. Doyle and A. Pavel ⑤ | G. Doyle and A. Pavel ⑤  4-6, 6-3, 6-3 | G. Doyle and A. Pavel ⑤  6-4, 6-3 | | |
| 18  B. Dunn and V. Spadea | | | | |
| 19  G. Diaz and L. Olguin | J. Delgado and T. H. Henman  6-7(1-7), 6-4, 6-3 | | E. Abaroa and A. Radulescu ④  3-6, 6-3, 6-4 | |
| 20  J. Delgado and T. H. Henman | | | | |
| 21  J. Greenhalgh and C. A. Reano | J. Greenhalgh and C. A. Reano  4-6, 4-6, 6-4 | E. Abaroa and A. Radulescu ④  6-7(5-7), 6-3, 6-2 | | |
| 22  P. Braga and G. Fernandes | | | | |
| 23  B. Jacob and D. Miketa | E. Abaroa and A. Radulescu ④  7-6(7-3), 6-4 | | | S. Baldas and S. Draper ③  6-1, 4-6, 9-7 |
| 24  E. Abaroa and A. Radulescu ④ | | | | |
| 25  D. J. Sanders and M. Schofield ⑧ | D. J. Sanders and M. Schofield ⑧  w/o | M. Bhupathi and N. Kirtane  7-5, 4-6, 6-3 | | |
| 26  S. Adbib and T. Harel Ben Simon | | | | |
| 27  J. J. Esqueda and G. Silberstein | M. Bhupathi and N. Kirtane  6-1, 6-2 | | M. Bhupathi and N. Kirtane  7-5, 6-3 | |
| 28  M. Bhupathi and N. Kirtane | | | | |
| 29  L. Ilou and S. Ladipo | L. Ilou and S. Ladipo  7-6(7-4), 4-6, 7-5 | L. Ilou and S. Ladipo  6-3, 6-4 | | |
| 30  S. S. Koehler and H.-K. Song | | | | |
| 31  S. Chukhan and S. Yongchantanasakul | G. A. Degreef and A. Zingman ②  6-4, 6-2 | | | |
| 32  G. A. Degreef and A. Zingman ② | | | | |

Heavy type denotes seeded players. The encircled figure against names denotes the order in which they have been seeded. The Committee reserves the right to alter the seeding order in the event of withdrawals. The Matches will be the best of three sets.

# EVENT XI.—THE GIRLS' SINGLES CHAMPIONSHIP

The Winner will become the holder, for the year only, of a Cup presented by The All England Lawn Tennis and Croquet Club. The Winner and Runner-up will each receive a personal prize.

### FIRST ROUND

1 Miss M. Babel ① (GER)
2 Miss M. V. Benitez (PAR)
3 Miss K. Gyorke (HUN)
4 Miss T. H. Wainwright (GBR)
5 Miss L. Courtois (BEL)
6 Miss S. Duangchang (THA)
7 Miss J.-Y. Choi (KOR)
8 Miss A. Miller ⑮ (USA)
9 Miss C. Cristea ⑨ (ROM)
10 Miss S. Locher (SUI)
11 Miss A. M. H. Wainwright (GBR)
12 Miss Z. Nemsakova (TCH)
13 Miss M. Olave (URU)
14 Miss E. E. Jelfs (GBR)
15 Miss S. Burstein (ISR)
16 Miss A. Sugiyama ⑧ (JPN)
17 Miss P. Nelson ④ (USA)
18 Miss C. Dorey (FRA)
19 Miss D. Randriantefy (MAD)
20 Miss L. McShea (AUS)
21 Miss M. Chernovita (INA)
22 Miss L. A. Woodroffe (GBR)
23 Miss E. Gevers (RSA)
24 Miss M. Donoshiro ⑭ (JPN)
25 Miss N. Marra ⑪ (VEN)
26 Miss H. Mochizuki (JPN)
27 Miss A. Reddy (IND)
28 Miss A. Laso (ESP)
29 Miss B. Sangaram (THA)
30 Miss J. M. Pullin (GBR)
31 Miss M. F. Landa (ARG)
32 Miss R. De Los Rios ⑥ (PAR)
33 Miss A. Smashnova ⑤ (ISR)
34 Miss C. P. McCarthy (IRL)
35 Miss F. M. La'O (PHI)
36 Miss K. Takuma (JPN)
37 Miss L. Jansson (FIN)
38 Miss S.-A. Siddall (GBR)
39 Miss S. Mingmolee (THA)
40 Miss L. Richterova ② (TCH)
41 Miss L. Schaerer ⑬ (PAR)
42 Miss Y. Rodriguez (MEX)
43 Miss N. Joshi (IND)
44 Miss L. Horn (RSA)
45 Miss A. Glass (GBR)
46 Miss S. S. Tse (GBR)
47 Miss Y. Tanaka (JPN)
48 Miss L. Davenport ③ (USA)
49 Miss N. Feber ⑦ (BEL)
50 Miss T. Tanasukarn (THA)
51 Miss D. Sutedja (INA)
52 Miss M. Avotins (AUS)
53 Miss L. Z. Nhavene (MOZ)
54 Miss L. A. Ahl (GBR)
55 Miss R. Grande (ITA)
56 Miss E. Likhovtseva ⑩ (CIS)
57 Miss J. Steven ⑯ (USA)
58 Miss S. Chartsuthiphan (THA)
59 Miss M. Muric (CRO)
60 Miss V. Valdovinos (PAR)
61 Miss K. M. Cross (GBR)
62 Miss S. Jeyaseelan (CAN)
63 Miss G. Gutierrez (COL)
64 Miss C. Rubin ② (USA)

### SECOND ROUND

Miss M. Babel ① — 6-1, 6-2
Miss K. Gyorke — 2-6, 6-3, 6-3
Miss L. Courtois — 6-1, 6-3
Miss A. Miller ⑮ — 6-1, 6-1
Miss C. Cristea ⑨ — 6-2, 6-4
Miss Z. Nemsakova — 7-6(7-4), 6-2
Miss E. E. Jelfs — 6-0, 6-1
Miss A. Sugiyama ⑧ — 6-7(5-7), 6-3, 6-0
Miss P. Nelson ④ — 6-4, 6-3
Miss L. McShea — 6-2, 7-6(7-2)
Miss M. Chernovita — 6-1, 6-4
Miss M. Donoshiro ⑭ — 6-3, 7-5
Miss H. Mochizuki — 3-6, 6-2, 7-5
Miss A. Laso — 6-4, 7-6(7-3)
Miss J. M. Pullin — 6-3, 6-1
Miss R. De Los Rios ⑥ — 5-7, 6-1, 8-6
Miss A. Smashnova ⑤ — 6-1, 6-1
Miss K. Takuma — 6-3, 7-6(7-4)
Miss S.-A. Siddall — 6-1, 6-2
Miss S. Mingmolee — 6-2, 6-3
Miss L. Schaerer ⑬ — 6-3, 6-4
Miss L. Horn — 6-4, 6-2
Miss A. Glass — 7-5, 6-2
Miss L. Davenport ③ — 6-2, 7-6(7-3)
Miss N. Feber ⑦ — 6-0, 6-2
Miss M. Avotins — 6-1, 6-3
Miss L. Z. Nhavene — 6-4, 4-6, 7-5
Miss E. Likhovtseva ⑩ — 6-2, 6-3
Miss J. Steven ⑯ — 6-0, 6-1
Miss V. Valdovinos — 6-0, 6-3
Miss S. Jeyaseelan — 6-4, 6-2
Miss C. Rubin ② — 6-3, 6-1

### THIRD ROUND

Miss M. Babel ① — 6-0, 6-0
Miss L. Courtois — 6-2, 6-0
Miss C. Cristea ⑨ — 6-4, 6-0
Miss A. Sugiyama ⑧ — 2-6, 6-4, 8-6
Miss L. McShea — 6-1, 6-4
Miss M. Donoshiro ⑭ — 6-1, 6-2
Miss H. Mochizuki — 6-3, 6-3
Miss R. De Los Rios ⑥ — 7-5, 6-1
Miss A. Smashnova ⑤ — 6-1, 6-0
Miss S.-A. Siddall — 6-1, 6-1
Miss L. Schaerer ⑬ — 7-6(7-1), 7-5
Miss A. Glass — 6-4, 6-2
Miss N. Feber ⑦ — 6-2, 6-1
Miss E. Likhovtseva ⑩ — 7-6(7-5), 6-2
Miss J. Steven ⑯ — 6-1, 6-1
Miss C. Rubin ② — 6-1, 6-3

### QUARTER-FINALS

Miss L. Courtois — 6-4, 7-6(7-2)
Miss A. Sugiyama ⑧ — 6-4, 0-6, 6-1
Miss M. Donoshiro ⑭ — 6-4, 2-6, 6-4
Miss R. De Los Rios ⑥ — 6-2, 3-6, 6-4
Miss A. Smashnova ⑤ — 6-3, 6-0
Miss A. Glass — 6-4, 6-2
Miss E. Likhovtseva ⑩ — 6-2, 4-6, 8-6
Miss C. Rubin ② — 6-1, 6-2

### SEMI-FINALS

Miss L. Courtois — 7-6(8-6), 6-3
Miss R. De Los Rios ⑥ — 6-4, 6-4
Miss A. Glass — 3-6, 6-4, 6-2
Miss C. Rubin ② — 6-4, 6-4

### FINAL

Miss L. Courtois — 7-6(7-4), 4-6, 6-4
Miss C. Rubin ② — 6-1, 6-7(5-7), 8-6

### Winner

Miss C. Rubin ② — 6-2, 7-5

Heavy type denotes seeded players. The encircled figure against names denotes the order in which they have been seeded. The Committee reserves the right to alter the seeding order in the event of withdrawals. The Matches will be the best of three sets.

---

# EVENT XII.—THE GIRLS' DOUBLES CHAMPIONSHIP

Holders: Miss C. BARCLAY and Miss L. ZALTZ

The Winners will become the holders, for the year only, of a Cup presented by The All England Lawn Tennis and Croquet Club. The Winners and Runners-up will each receive a personal prize.

### FIRST ROUND

1 Miss L. Courtois and Miss N. Feber ①
2 Miss M. Chernovita and Miss F. M. La'O
3 Miss S. Jeyaseelan and Miss E. Likhovtseva
4 Miss C. Cristea and Miss S. S. Tse
5 Miss L. Jansson and Miss M. Muric
6 Miss S. Chartsuthiphan and Miss T. Tanasukarn
7 Miss Z. Hearn and Miss Z. Mellis
8 Miss M. F. Landa and Miss N. Marra ⑤
9 Miss Z. Nemsakova and Miss L. Richterova ③
10 Miss L. A. Ahl and Miss S.-A. Siddall
11 Miss H. Mochizuki and Miss Y. Tanaka
12 Miss A. Glass and Miss A. Smashnova
13 Miss S. Mingmolee and Miss D. Sutedja
14 Miss R. M. Hughes and Miss A. M. H. Wainwright
15 Miss N. Joshi and Miss A. Reddy
16 Miss P. Nelson and Miss J. Steven ⑦
17 Miss R. De Los Rios and Miss L. Schaerer ⑧
18 Miss L. Z. Nhavene and Miss Y. Rodriguez
19 Miss J. M. Pullin and Miss L. A. Woodroffe
20 Miss J.-Y. Choi and Miss K. Takuma
21 Miss S. Duangchang and Miss B. Sangaram
22 Miss C. P. McCarthy and Miss V. Valdovinos
23 Miss G. Gutierrez and Miss M. Miller
24 Miss M. Avotins and Miss L. McShea ④
25 Miss M. Donoshiro and Miss A. Sugiyama ⑥
26 Miss K. M. Cross and Miss T. H. Wainwright
27 Miss C. Dorey and Miss D. Randriantefy
28 Miss M. V. Benitez and Miss M. Olave
29 Miss E. E. Jelfs and Miss C. Taylor
30 Miss S. Burstein and Miss S. Locher
31 Miss E. Gevers and Miss L. Horn
32 Miss L. Davenport and Miss C. Rubin ②

### SECOND ROUND

Miss L. Courtois and Miss N. Feber ① — 6-2, 6-1
Miss S. Jeyaseelan and Miss E. Likhovtseva — 6-3, 4-6, 6-3
Miss L. Jansson and Miss M. Muric — 6-2, 6-2
Miss M. F. Landa and Miss N. Marra ⑤ — 6-1, 6-4
Miss Z. Nemsakova and Miss L. Richterova ③ — 6-3, 6-2
Miss H. Mochizuki and Miss Y. Tanaka — 3-6, 6-2, 6-1
Miss R. M. Hughes and Miss A. M. H. Wainwright — 6-0, 6-3
Miss P. Nelson and Miss J. Steven ⑦ — 6-4, 6-2
Miss R. De Los Rios and Miss L. Schaerer ⑧ — 5-7, 6-2, 6-3
Miss J. M. Pullin and Miss L. A. Woodroffe — 2-6, 7-6(7-3), 6-1
Miss S. Duangchang and Miss B. Sangaram
Miss M. Avotins and Miss L. McShea ④ — 6-2, 6-0
Miss M. Donoshiro and Miss A. Sugiyama ⑥ — 7-5, 6-3
Miss C. Dorey and Miss D. Randriantefy — 6-3, 1-6, 6-4
Miss E. E. Jelfs and Miss C. Taylor — 6-2, 6-3
Miss E. Gevers and Miss L. Horn — w/o

### QUARTER-FINALS

Miss L. Courtois and Miss N. Feber ① — w/o
Miss M. F. Landa and Miss N. Marra ⑤ — w/o
Miss H. Mochizuki and Miss Y. Tanaka — 7-6(7-4), 7-5
Miss P. Nelson and Miss J. Steven ⑦ — 6-3, 6-0
Miss J. M. Pullin and Miss L. A. Woodroffe — 7-5, 4-6, 7-5
Miss M. Avotins and Miss L. McShea ④ — 6-4, 6-3
Miss C. Dorey and Miss D. Randriantefy — w/o
Miss E. Gevers and Miss L. Horn — 2-6, 6-3, 6-4

### SEMI-FINALS

Miss L. Courtois and Miss N. Feber ① — 6-1, 6-3
Miss P. Nelson and Miss J. Steven ⑦ — 6-4, 6-1
Miss M. Avotins and Miss L. McShea ④ — 4-6, 6-1, 6-2
Miss E. Gevers and Miss L. Horn — 6-3, 3-6, 6-0

### FINAL

Miss P. Nelson and Miss J. Steven ⑦ — 3-6, 6-4, 11-9
Miss M. Avotins and Miss L. McShea ④

### Winners

Miss M. Avotins and Miss L. McShea ④ — 2-6, 6-4, 6-3

Heavy type denotes seeded players. The encircled figure against names denotes the order in which they have been seeded. The Committee reserves the right to alter the seeding order in the event of withdrawals. The Matches will be the best of three sets.

---

## COUNTRIES IN THIS YEARS CHAMPIONSHIPS
# ABBREVIATIONS

| | | | |
|---|---|---|---|
| ARG Argentina | CRO Croatia | NZL New Zealand | THA Thailand |
| AUS Australia | TCH Czechoslovakia | NGR Nigeria | UKR Ukraine |
| AUT Austria | FIN Finland | ISR Israel | PRY Paraguay | URU Uruguay |
| BAH Bahamas | FRA France | ITA Italy | PER Peru | URY Uruguay |
| BEL Belgium | GEO Georgia | CIV Ivory Coast | PHI Philippines | USA United States |
| BRA Brazil | GER Germany | JPN Japan | POL Poland | VEN Venezuela |
| BUL Bulgaria | GBR Great Britain | KEN Kenya | ROM Romania | YUG Yugoslavia |
| CAN Canada | HKG Hong Kong | KOR Korea, Republic of | SLO Slovenia | ZWE Zimbabwe |
| CHI Chile | HUN Hungary | LAT Latvia | RSA South Africa | |
| CHN China | IND India | MAD Madagascar | ESP Spain | |
| COL Columbia | INA Indonesia | MEX Mexico | SWE Sweden | |
| CIS Commonwealth of Independent States | IRL Ireland | MAR Morocco | SUI Switzerland | |
| | | MOZ Mozambique | | |
| | | NED Netherlands | | |

# THE CHAMPIONSHIP ROLL
## Champions and Runners-up

## MEN'S SINGLES

1877—S. W. Gore
    *W. C. Marshall*
1878—P. F. Hadow
    *S. W. Gore*
★1879—J. T. Hartley
    *V. St. L. Goold*
1880—J. T. Hartley
    *H. F. Lawford*
1881—W. Renshaw
    *J. T. Hartley*
1882—W. Renshaw
    *E. Renshaw*
1883—W. Renshaw
    *E. Renshaw*
1884—W. Renshaw
    *H. F. Lawford*
1885—W. Renshaw
    *H. F. Lawford*
1886—W. Renshaw
    *H. F. Lawford*
★1887—H. F. Lawford
    *E. Renshaw*
1888—E. Renshaw
    *H. F. Lawford*
1889—W. Renshaw
    *E. Renshaw*
1890—W. J. Hamilton
    *W. Renshaw*
★1891—W. Baddeley
    *J. Pim*
1892—W. Baddeley
    *J. Pim*
1893—J. Pim
    *W. Baddeley*
1894—J. Pim
    *W. Baddeley*
★1895—W. Baddeley
    *W. V. Eaves*
1896—H. S. Mahony
    *W. Baddeley*

1897—R. F. Doherty
    *H. S. Mahony*
1898—R. F. Doherty
    *H. L. Doherty*
1899—R. F. Doherty
    *A. W. Gore*
1900—R. F. Doherty
    *S. H. Smith*
1901—A. W. Gore
    *R. F. Doherty*
1902—H. L. Doherty
    *A. W. Gore*
1903—H. L. Doherty
    *F. L. Riseley*
1904—H. L. Doherty
    *F. L. Riseley*
1905—H. L. Doherty
    *N. E. Brookes*
1906—H. L. Doherty
    *F. L. Riseley*
★1907—N. E. Brookes
    *A. W. Gore*
★1908—A. W. Gore
    *H. Roper Barrett*
1909—A. W. Gore
    *M. J. G. Ritchie*
1910—A. F. Wilding
    *A. W. Gore*

1911—A. F. Wilding
    *H. Roper Barrett*
1912—A. F. Wilding
    *A. W. Gore*
1913—A. F. Wilding
    *M. E. McLoughlin*
1914—N. E. Brookes
    *A. F. Wilding*
1919—G. L. Patterson
    *N. E. Brookes*
1920—W. T. Tilden
    *G. L. Patterson*
1921—W. T. Tilden
    *B. I. C. Norton*
★†1922—G. L. Patterson
    *R. Lycett*
1923—W. M. Johnston
    *F. T. Hunter*
1924—J. Borotra
    *R. Lacoste*
1925—R. Lacoste
    *J. Borotra*
1926—J. Borotra
    *H. Kinsey*
1927—H. Cochet
    *J. Borotra*
1928—R. Lacoste
    *H. Cochet*

1929—H. Cochet
    *J. Borotra*
1930—W. T. Tilden
    *W. Allison*
1931—S. B. Wood
    *F. X. Shields*
1932—H. E. Vines
    *H. W. Austin*
1933—J. H. Crawford
    *H. E. Vines*
1934—F. J. Perry
    *J. H. Crawford*
1935—F. J. Perry
    *G. von Cramm*
1936—F. J. Perry
    *G. von Cramm*
★1937—J. D. Budge
    *G. von Cramm*
1938—J. D. Budge
    *H. W. Austin*
★1939—R. L. Riggs
    *E. T. Cooke*
★1946—Y. Petra
    *G. E. Brown*
1947—J. Kramer
    *T. Brown*
★1948—R. Falkenburg
    *J. E. Bromwich*
1949—F. R. Schroeder
    *J. Drobny*
★1950—B. Patty
    *F. A. Sedgman*
1951—R. Savitt
    *K. McGregor*
1952—F. A. Sedgman
    *J. Drobny*
★1953—V. Seixas
    *K. Nielsen*
1954—J. Drobny
    *K. R. Rosewall*

1955—T. Trabert
    *K. Nielsen*
★1956—L. A. Hoad
    *K. R. Rosewall*
1957—L. A. Hoad
    *A. J. Cooper*
★1958—A. J. Cooper
    *N. A. Fraser*
★1959—A. Olmedo
    *R. Laver*
★1960—N. A. Fraser
    *R. Laver*
1961—R. Laver
    *C. R. McKinley*
1962—R. Laver
    *M. F. Mulligan*
★1963—C. R. McKinley
    *F. S. Stolle*
1964—R. Emerson
    *F. S. Stolle*
1965—R. Emerson
    *F. S. Stolle*
1966—M. Santana
    *R. D. Ralston*
1967—J. D. Newcombe
    *W. P. Bungert*
1968—R. Laver
    *A. D. Roche*
1969—R. Laver
    *J. D. Newcombe*
1970—J. D. Newcombe
    *K. R. Rosewall*
1971—J. D. Newcombe
    *S. R. Smith*
★1972—S. R. Smith
    *I. Nastase*
★1973—J. Kodes
    *A. Metreveli*
1974—J. S. Connors
    *K. R. Rosewall*

1975—A. R. Ashe
    *J. S. Connors*
1976—B. Borg
    *I. Nastase*
1977—B. Borg
    *J. S. Connors*
1978—B. Borg
    *J. S. Connors*
1979—B. Borg
    *R. Tanner*
1980—B. Borg
    *J. P. McEnroe*
1981—J. P. McEnroe
    *B. Borg*
1982—J. S. Connors
    *J. P. McEnroe*
1983—J. P. McEnroe
    *C. J. Lewis*
1984—J. P. McEnroe
    *J. S. Connors*
1985—B. Becker
    *K. Curren*
1986—B. Becker
    *I. Lendl*
1987—P. Cash
    *I. Lendl*
1988—S. Edberg
    *B. Becker*
1989—B. Becker
    *S. Edberg*
1990—S. Edberg
    *B. Becker*
1991—M. Stich
    *B. Becker*
1992—A. Agassi
    *G. Ivanisevic*

## MEN'S DOUBLES

1879—L. R. Erskine and H. F. Lawford
    *F. Durant and G. E. Tabor*
1880—W. Renshaw and E. Renshaw
    *O. E. Woodhouse and C. J. Cole*
1881—W. Renshaw and E. Renshaw
    *W. J. Down and H. Vaughan*
1882—J. T. Hartley and R. T. Richardson
    *J. G. Horn and C. B. Russell*
1883—C. W. Grinstead and C. E. Welldon
    *C. B. Russell and R. T. Milford*
1884—W. Renshaw and E. Renshaw
    *E. W. Lewis and E. L. Williams*
1885—W. Renshaw and E. Renshaw
    *C. E. Farrar and A. J. Stanley*
1886—W. Renshaw and E. Renshaw
    *C. E. Farrar and A. J. Stanley*
1887—P. Bowes-Lyon and H. W. W. Wilberforce
    *J. H. Crispe and Barratt Smith*
1888—W. Renshaw and E. Renshaw
    *P. Bowes-Lyon and H. W. W. Wilberforce*
1889—W. Renshaw and E. Renshaw
    *E. W. Lewis and G. W. Hillyard*
1890—J. Pim and F. O. Stoker
    *E. W. Lewis and G. W. Hillyard*
1891—W. Baddeley and H. Baddeley
    *J Pim and F. O. Stoker*
1892—H. S. Barlow and E. W. Lewis
    *W. Baddeley and H. Baddeley*
1893—J. Pim and F. O. Stoker
    *E. W. Lewis and H. S. Barlow*
1894—W. Baddeley and H. Baddeley
    *H. S. Barlow and C. H. Martin*
1895—W. Baddeley and H. Baddeley
    *E. W. Lewis and W. V. Eaves*
1896—W. Baddeley and H. Baddeley
    *R. F. Doherty and H. A. Nisbet*
1897—R. F. Doherty and H. L. Doherty
    *W. Baddeley and H. Baddeley*
1898—R. F. Doherty and H. L. Doherty
    *H. A. Nisbet and C. Hobart*
1899—R. F. Doherty and H. L. Doherty
    *H. A. Nisbet and C. Hobart*
1900—R. F. Doherty and H. L. Doherty
    *H. Roper Barrett and H. A. Nisbet*
1901—R. F. Doherty and H. L. Doherty
    *Dwight Davis and Holcombe Ward*
1902—S. H. Smith and F. L. Riseley
    *R. F. Doherty and H. L. Doherty*
1903—R. F. Doherty and H. L. Doherty
    *S. H. Smith and F. L. Riseley*
1904—R. F. Doherty and H. L. Doherty
    *S. H. Smith and F. L. Riseley*
1905—R. F. Doherty and H. L. Doherty
    *S. H. Smith and F. L. Riseley*
1906—S. H. Smith and F. L. Riseley
    *R. F. Doherty and H. L. Doherty*
1907—N. E. Brookes and A. F. Wilding
    *B. C. Wright and C. K. Behr*
1908—A. F. Wilding and M. J. G. Ritchie
    *A. W. Gore and H. Roper Barrett*
1909—A. W. Gore and H. Roper Barrett
    *S. N. Doust and H. A. Parker*
1910—A. F. Wilding and M. J. G. Ritchie
    *A. W. Gore and H. Roper Barrett*
1911—M. Decugis and A. H. Gobert
    *M. J. G. Ritchie and A. F. Wilding*
1912—H. Roper Barrett and C. P. Dixon
    *M. Decugis and A. H. Gobert*
1913—H. Roper Barrett and C. P. Dixon
    *F. W. Rahe and H. Kleinschroth*

1914—N. E. Brookes and A. F. Wilding
    *H. Roper Barrett and C. P. Dixon*
1919—R. V. Thomas and P. O'Hara-Wood
    *R. Lycett and R. W. Heath*
1920—R. N. Williams and C. S. Garland
    *A. R. F. Kingscote and J. C. Parke*
1921—R. Lycett and M. Woosnam
    *F. G. Lowe and A. H. Lowe*
† 1922—R. Lycett and J. O. Anderson
    *G. L. Patterson and P. O'Hara-Wood*
1923—R. Lycett and L. A. Godfree
    *Count de Gomar and E. Flaquer*
1924—F. T. Hunter and V. Richards
    *R. N. Williams and W. M. Washburn*
1925—J. Borotra and R. Lacoste
    *J. Hennessey and R. Casey*
1926—H. Cochet and J. Brugnon
    *V. Richards and H. Kinsey*
1927—F. T. Hunter and W. T. Tilden
    *J. Brugnon and H. Cochet*
1928—H. Cochet and J. Brugnon
    *G. L. Patterson and J. B. Hawkes*
1929—W. Allison and J. Van Ryn
    *J. C. Gregory and I. G. Collins*
1930—W. Allison and J. Van Ryn
    *J. H. Doeg and G. M. Lott*
1931—G. M. Lott and J. Van Ryn
    *H. Cochet and J. Brugnon*
1932—J. Borotra and J. Brugnon
    *G. P. Hughes and F. J. Perry*
1933—J. Borotra and J. Brugnon
    *R. Nunoi and J. Satoh*
1934—G. M. Lott and L. R. Stoefen
    *J. Borotra and J. Brugnon*
1935—J. H. Crawford and A. K. Quist
    *W. Allison and J. Van Ryn*
1936—G. P. Hughes and C. R. D. Tuckey
    *C. E. Hare and F. H. D. Wilde*
1937—J. D. Budge and G. Mako
    *G. P. Hughes and C. R. D. Tuckey*
1938—J. D. Budge and G. Mako
    *H. Henkel and G. von Metaxa*
1939—R. L. Riggs and E. T. Cooke
    *C. E. Hare and F. H. D. Wilde*
1946—T. Brown and J. Kramer
    *G. E. Brown and D. Pails*
1947—R. Falkenburg and J. Kramer
    *A. J. Mottram and O. W. Sidwell*
1948—J. E. Bromwich and F. A. Sedgman
    *T. Brown and G. Mulloy*
1949—R. Gonzales and F. Parker
    *G. Mulloy and F. R. Schroeder*
1950—J. E. Bromwich and A. K. Quist
    *G. E. Brown and O. W. Sidwell*
1951—K. McGregor and F. A. Sedgman
    *J. Drobny and E. W. Sturgess*
1952—K. McGregor and F. A. Sedgman
    *V. Seixas and E. W. Sturgess*
1953—L. A. Hoad and K. R. Rosewall
    *R. N. Hartwig and M. G. Rose*
1954—R. N. Hartwig and M. G. Rose
    *V. Seixas and T. Trabert*
1955—R. N. Hartwig and L. A. Hoad
    *N. A. Fraser and K. R. Rosewall*
1956—L. A. Hoad and K. R. Rosewall
    *N. Pietrangeli and O. Sirola*
1957—G. Mulloy and B. Patty
    *N. A. Fraser and L. A. Hoad*
1958—S. Davidson and U. Schmidt
    *A. J. Cooper and N. A. Fraser*

1959—R. Emerson and N. A. Fraser
    *R. Laver and R. Mark*
1960—R. H. Osuna and R. D. Ralston
    *M. G. Davies and R. K. Wilson*
1961—R. Emerson and N. A. Fraser
    *R. A. J. Hewitt and F. S. Stolle*
1962—R. A. J. Hewitt and F. S. Stolle
    *B. Jovanovic and N. Pilic*
1963—R. H. Osuna and A. Palafox
    *J. C. Barclay and P. Darmon*
1964—R. A. J. Hewitt and F. S. Stolle
    *R. Emerson and K. N. Fletcher*
1965—J. D. Newcombe and A. D. Roche
    *K. N. Fletcher and R. A. J. Hewitt*
1966—K. N. Fletcher and J. D. Newcombe
    *W. W. Bowrey and O. K. Davidson*
1967—R. A. J. Hewitt and F. D. McMillan
    *R. Emerson and K. N. Fletcher*
1968—J. D. Newcombe and A. D. Roche
    *K. R. Rosewall and F. S. Stolle*
1969—J. D. Newcombe and A. D. Roche
    *T. S. Okker and M. C. Riessen*
1970—J. D. Newcombe and A. D. Roche
    *K. R. Rosewall and F. S. Stolle*
1971—R. S. Emerson and R. G. Laver
    *A. R. Ashe and R. D. Ralston*
1972—R. A. J. Hewitt and F. D. McMillan
    *S. R. Smith and E. J. van Dillen*
1973—J. S. Connors and I. Nastase
    *J. R. Cooper and N. A. Fraser*
1974—J. D. Newcombe and A. D. Roche
    *R. C. Lutz and S. R. Smith*
1975—V. Gerulaitis and A. Mayer
    *C. Dowdeswell and A. J. Stone*
1976—B. E. Gottfried and R. Ramirez
    *R. L. Case and G. Masters*
1977—R. L. Case and G. Masters
    *J. G. Alexander and P. C. Dent*
1978—R. A. J. Hewitt and F. D. McMillan
    *P. Fleming and J. P. McEnroe*
1979—P. Fleming and J. P. McEnroe
    *B. E. Gottfried and R. Ramirez*
1980—P. McNamara and P. McNamee
    *R. C. Lutz and S. R. Smith*
1981—P. Fleming and J. P. McEnroe
    *R. C. Lutz and S. R. Smith*
1982—P. McNamara and P. McNamee
    *P. Fleming and J. P. McEnroe*
1983—P. Fleming and J. P. McEnroe
    *T. E. Gullikson and T. R. Gullikson*
1984—P. Fleming and J. P. McEnroe
    *P. Cash and P. McNamee*
1985—H. P. Guenthardt and B. Taroczy
    *P. Cash and J. B. Fitzgerald*
1986—J. Nystrom and M. Wilander
    *G. Donnelly and P. Fleming*
1987—K. Flach and R. Seguso
    *S. Casal and E. Sanchez*
1988—K. Flach and R. Seguso
    *J. B. Fitzgerald and A. Jarryd*
1989—J. B. Fitzgerald and A. Jarryd
    *R. Leach and J. Pugh*
1990—R. Leach and J. Pugh
    *P. Aldrich and D. T. Visser*
1991—J. B. Fitzgerald and A. Jarryd
    *J. Frana and L. Lavalle*
1992—J. P. McEnroe and M. Stich
    *J. Grabb and R. A. Reneberg*

# THE CHAMPIONSHIP ROLL

## LADIES' SINGLES

1884—Miss M. Watson
*Miss Watson*
1885—Miss M. Watson
*Miss B. Bingley*
1886—Miss B. Bingley
*Miss M. Watson*
1887—Miss L. Dod
*Miss B. Bingley*
1888—Miss L. Dod
*Mrs. G. W. Hillyard*
★1889—Mrs G. W. Hillyard
*Miss L. Rice*
★1890—Miss L. Rice
*Miss Jacks*
★1891—Miss L. Dod
*Mrs. G. W. Hillyard*
1892—Miss L. Dod
*Mrs. G. W. Hillyard*
1893—Miss L. Dod
*Mrs. G. W. Hillyard*
★1894—Mrs. G. W. Hillyard
*Miss Austin*
★1895—Miss C. Cooper
*Miss Jackson*
1896—Miss C. Cooper
*Mrs. Pickering*
1897—Mrs. G. W. Hillyard
*Miss C. Cooper*
★1898—Miss C. Cooper
*Miss Martin*
1899—Mrs. G. W. Hillyard
*Miss C. Cooper*
1900—Mrs. G. W. Hillyard
*Miss C. Cooper*
1901—Mrs. A. Sterry
*Mrs. G. W. Hillyard*
1902—Miss M. E. Robb
*Mrs. A. Sterry*
★1903—Miss D. K. Douglass
*Miss E. W. Thomson*
1904—Miss D. K. Douglass
*Mrs. A. Sterry*

1905—Miss M. Sutton
*Miss D. K. Douglass*
1906—Miss D. K. Douglass
*Miss M. Sutton*
1907—Miss M. Sutton
*Mrs. Lambert Chambers*
★1908—Mrs. A. Sterry
*Miss A. M. Morton*
★1909—Miss D. P. Boothby
*Miss A. M. Morton*
1910—Mrs. Lambert Chambers
*Miss D. P. Boothby*
1911—Mrs. Lambert Chambers
*Miss D. P. Boothby*
★1912—Mrs. D. R. Larcombe
*Mrs. A. Sterry*
★1913—Mrs. Lambert Chambers
*Mrs. R. J. McNair*
1914—Mrs. Lambert Chambers
*Mrs. D. R. Larcombe*
1919—Mlle. S. Lenglen
*Mrs. Lambert Chambers*
1920—Mlle. S. Lenglen
*Mrs. Lambert Chambers*
1921—Mlle. S. Lenglen
*Miss E. Ryan*
† 1922—Mlle. S. Lenglen
*Mrs. Mallory*
1923—Mlle. S. Lenglen
*Miss K. McKane*
1924—Miss K. McKane
*Miss H. Wills*
1925—Mlle. S. Lenglen
*Miss J. Fry*
1926—Mrs. L. A. Godfree
*Sta. L. de Alvarez*
1927—Miss H. Wills
*Sta. L. de Alvarez*
1928—Miss H. Wills
*Sta. L. de Alvarez*
1929—Miss H. Wills
*Miss H. H. Jacobs*

1930—Mrs. F. S. Moody
*Miss E. Ryan*
★1931—Fraulein C. Aussem
*Fraulein H. Krahwinkel*
1932—Mrs. F. S. Moody
*Miss H. H. Jacobs*
1933—Mrs. F. S. Moody
*Miss D. E. Round*
★1934—Miss D. E. Round
*Miss H. H. Jacobs*
1935—Mrs. F. S. Moody
*Miss H. H. Jacobs*
★1936—Miss H. H. Jacobs
*Frau. S. Sperling*
1937—Miss D. E. Round
*Miss J. Jedrzejowska*
★1938—Mrs. F. S. Moody
*Miss H. H. Jacobs*
★1939—Miss A. Marble
*Miss K. E. Stammers*
★1946—Miss P. Betz
*Miss L. Brough*
★1947—Miss M. Osborne
*Miss D. Hart*
1948—Miss L. Brough
*Miss D. Hart*
1949—Miss L. Brough
*Mrs. W. du Pont*
1950—Miss L. Brough
*Mrs. W. du Pont*
1951—Miss D. Hart
*Miss S. Fry*
1952—Miss M. Connolly
*Miss L. Brough*
1953—Miss M. Connolly
*Miss D. Hart*
1954—Miss M. Connolly
*Miss L. Brough*
★1955—Miss L. Brough
*Mrs. J. Fleitz*
1956—Miss S. Fry
*Miss A. Buxton*

★1957—Miss A. Gibson
*Miss D. R. Hard*
1958—Miss A. Gibson
*Miss A. Mortimer*
★1959—Miss M. E. Bueno
*Miss D. R. Hard*
1960—Miss M. E. Bueno
*Miss S. Reynolds*
★1961—Miss A. Mortimer
*Miss C. C. Truman*
1962—Mrs. J. R. Susman
*Mrs. V. Sukova*
★1963—Miss M. Smith
*Miss B. J. Moffitt*
1964—Miss M. E. Bueno
*Miss M. Smith*
1965—Miss M. Smith
*Miss M. E. Bueno*
1966—Mrs. L. W. King
*Miss M. E. Bueno*
1967—Mrs. L. W. King
*Mrs. P. F. Jones*
1968—Mrs. L. W. King
*Miss J. A. M. Tegart*
1969—Mrs. P. F. Jones
*Mrs. L. W. King*
★1970—Mrs. B. M. Court
*Mrs. L. W. King*
1971—Miss E. F. Goolagong
*Mrs. B. M. Court*
1972—Mrs. L. W. King
*Miss E. F. Goolagong*
1973—Mrs. L. W. King
*Miss C. M. Evert*

1974—Miss C. M. Evert
*Mrs. O. Morozova*
1975—Mrs. L. W. King
*Mrs. R. Cawley*
★1976—Miss C. M. Evert
*Mrs. R. Cawley*
1977—Miss S. V. Wade
*Miss B. F. Stove*
1978—Miss M. Navratilova
*Miss C. M. Evert*
1979—Miss M. Navratilova
*Mrs. J. M. Lloyd*
1980—Mrs. R. Cawley
*Mrs. J. M. Lloyd*
1981—Mrs. J. M. Lloyd
*Miss H. Mandlikova*
1982—Miss M. Navratilova
*Mrs. J. M. Lloyd*
1983—Miss M. Navratilova
*Miss A. Jaeger*
1984—Miss M. Navratilova
*Mrs. J. M. Lloyd*
1985—Miss M. Navratilova
*Mrs. J. M. Lloyd*
1986—Miss M. Navratilova
*Miss H. Mandlikova*
1987—Miss M. Navratilova
*Miss S. Graf*
1988—Miss S. Graf
*Miss M. Navratilova*
1989—Miss S. Graf
*Miss M. Navratilova*
1990—Miss M. Navratilova
*Miss Z. L. Garrison*
1991—Miss S. Graf
*Miss G. Sabatini*
1992—Miss S. Graf
*Miss M. Seles*

## LADIES' DOUBLES

1913—Mrs. R. J. McNair and Miss D. P. Boothby
*Mrs. A. Sterry and Mrs. Lambert Chambers*
1914—Miss E. Ryan and Miss A. M. Morton
*Mrs. D. R. Larcombe and Mrs. Hannam*
1919—Mlle. S. Lenglen and Miss E. Ryan
*Mrs. Lambert Chambers and Mrs. D. R. Larcombe*
1920—Mlle. S. Lenglen and Miss E. Ryan
*Mrs. Lambert Chambers and Mrs. D. R. Larcombe*
1921—Mlle. S. Lenglen and Miss E. Ryan
*Mrs. A. E. Beamish and Mrs. Peacock*
1922—Mlle. S. Lenglen and Miss E. Ryan
*Mrs. A. D. Stocks and Miss K. McKane*
1923—Mlle. S. Lenglen and Miss E. Ryan
*Miss J. Austin and Miss E. L. Colyer*
1924—Mrs. H. Wightman and Miss H. Wills
*Mrs. B. C. Covell and Miss K. McKane*
1925—Mlle. S. Lenglen and Miss E. Ryan
*Mrs. A. V. Bridge and Mrs. C. G. McIlquham*
1926—Miss E. Ryan and Miss M. K. Browne
*Mrs. L. A. Godfree and Miss E. L. Colyer*
1927—Miss H. Wills and Miss E. Ryan
*Miss E. L. Heine and Mrs. Peacock*
1928—Miss Holcroft-Watson and Miss P. Saunders
*Miss E. H. Harvey and Miss E. Bennett*
1929—Miss Holcroft-Watson and Mrs. L. R. C. Michell
*Mrs. B. C. Covell and Mrs. D. C. Shepherd-Barron*
1930—Mrs. F. S. Moody and Miss E. Ryan
*Miss E. Cross and Miss S. Palfrey*
1931—Mrs. D. C. Shepherd-Barron and Miss P. E. Mudford
*Mlle. D. Metaxa and Mlle. J. Sigart*
1932—Mlle. D. Metaxa and Mlle. J. Sigart
*Miss E. Ryan and Miss H. H. Jacobs*
1933—Mme. R. Mathieu and Miss E. Ryan
*Miss F. James and Miss A. M. Yorke*
1934—Mme. R. Mathieu and Miss E. Ryan
*Mrs. D. Andrus and Mme. Henrotin*
1935—Miss F. James and Miss K. E. Stammers
*Mme. R. Mathieu and Frau. S. Sperling*
1936—Miss F. James and Miss K. E. Stammers
*Mrs. S. P. Fabyan and Miss H. H. Jacobs*
1937—Mme. R. Mathieu and Miss A. M. Yorke
*Mrs. M. R. King and Mrs. J. B. Pittman*
1938—Mrs. S. P. Fabyan and Miss A. Marble
*Mme. R. Mathieu and Miss A. M. Yorke*
1939—Mrs. S. P. Fabyan and Miss A. Marble
*Miss H. H. Jacobs and Miss A. M. Yorke*
1946—Miss L. Brough and Miss M. Osborne
*Miss P. Betz and Miss D. Hart*

1947—Miss D. Hart and Mrs. P. C. Todd
*Miss L. Brough and Miss M. Osborne*
1948—Miss L. Brough and Mrs W. du Pont
*Miss D. Hart and Mrs. P. C. Todd*
1949—Miss L. Brough and Mrs. W. du Pont
*Miss G. Moran and Mrs. P. C. Todd*
1950—Miss L. Brough and Mrs. W. du Pont
*Miss S. Fry and Miss D. Hart*
1951—Miss S. Fry and Miss D. Hart
*Miss L. Brough and Mrs. W. du Pont*
1952—Miss S. Fry and Miss D. Hart
*Miss L. Brough and Miss M. Connolly*
1953—Miss S. Fry and Miss D. Hart
*Miss M. Connolly and Miss J. Sampson*
1954—Miss L. Brough and Mrs. W. du Pont
*Miss S. Fry and Miss D. Hart*
1955—Miss A. Mortimer and Miss J. A. Shilcock
*Miss S. J. Bloomer and Miss P. E. Ward*
1956—Miss A. Buxton and Miss A. Gibson
*Miss F. Muller and Miss D. G. Seeney*
1957—Miss A. Gibson and Miss D. R. Hard
*Mrs. K. Hawton and Mrs. T. D. Long*
1958—Miss M. E. Bueno and Miss A. Gibson
*Mrs. W. du Pont and Miss M. Varner*
1959—Miss J. Arth and Miss D. R. Hard
*Mrs. J. G. Fleitz and Miss C. C. Truman*
1960—Miss M. E. Bueno and Miss D. R. Hard
*Miss S. Reynolds and Miss R. Schuurman*
1961—Miss K. Hantze and Miss B. J. Moffitt
*Miss J. Lehane and Miss M. Smith*
1962—Miss B. J. Moffitt and Mrs. J. R. Susman
*Mrs. L. E. G. Price and Miss R. Schuurman*
1963—Miss M. E. Bueno and Miss D. R. Hard
*Miss R. A. Ebbern and Miss M. Smith*
1964—Miss M. Smith and Miss L. R. Turner
*Miss B. J. Moffitt and Mrs. J. R. Susman*
1965—Miss M. E. Bueno and Miss B. J. Moffitt
*Miss F. Durr and Miss J. Lieffrig*
1966—Miss M. E. Bueno and Miss N. Richey
*Miss M. Smith and Miss J. A. M. Tegart*
1967—Miss R. Casals and Mrs. L. W. King
*Miss M. E. Bueno and Miss N. Richey*
1968—Miss R. Casals and Mrs. L. W. King
*Miss F. Durr and Mrs. P. F. Jones*
1969—Mrs. B. M. Court and Miss J. A. M. Tegart
*Miss P. S. A. Hogan and Miss M. Michel*
1970—Miss R. Casals and Mrs. L. W. King
*Miss F. Durr and Miss S. V. Wade*

1971—Miss R. Casals and Mrs. L. W. King
*Mrs. B. M. Court and Miss E. F. Goolagong*
1972—Mrs. L. W. King and Miss B. F. Stove
*Mrs. D. E. Dalton and Miss F. Durr*
1973—Miss R. Casals and Mrs. L. W. King
*Miss F. Durr and Miss B. F. Stove*
1974—Miss E. F. Goolagong and Miss M. Michel
*Miss H. F. Gourlay and Miss K. M. Krantzcke*
1975—Miss A. K. Kiyomura and Miss K. Sawamatsu
*Miss F. Durr and Miss B. F. Stove*
1976—Miss C. M. Evert and Miss M. Navratilova
*Mrs. L. W. King and Miss B. F. Stove*
1977—Mrs. H. F. Gourlay Cawley and Miss J. C. Russell
*Miss M. Navratilova and Miss B. F. Stove*
1978—Miss G. E. Reid and Miss W. M. Turnbull
*Miss M. Jausovec and Miss V. Ruzici*
1979—Mrs. L. W. King and Miss M. Navratilova
*Miss B. F. Stove and Miss W. M. Turnbull*
1980—Miss K. Jordan and Miss A. E. Smith
*Miss R. Casals and Miss W. M. Turnbull*
1981—Miss M. Navratilova and Miss P. H. Shriver
*Miss K. Jordan and Miss A. E. Smith*
1982—Miss M. Navratilova and Miss P. H. Shriver
*Miss K. Jordan and Miss A. E. Smith*
1983—Miss M. Navratilova and Miss P. H. Shriver
*Miss R. Casals and Miss W. M. Turnbull*
1984—Miss M. Navratilova and Miss P. H. Shriver
*Miss K. Jordan and Miss A. E. Smith*
1985—Miss K. Jordan and Mrs. P. D. Smylie
*Miss M. Navratilova and Miss P. H. Shriver*
1986—Miss M. Navratilova and Miss P. H. Shriver
*Miss H. Mandlikova and Miss W. M. Turnbull*
1987—Miss C. Kohde-Kilsch and Miss H. Sukova
*Miss B. Nagelsen and Mrs. P. D. Smylie*
1988—Miss S. Graf and Miss G. Sabatini
*Miss L. Savchenko and Miss N. Zvereva*
1989—Miss J. Novotna and Miss H. Sukova
*Miss L. Savchenko and Miss N. Zvereva*
1990—Miss J. Novotna and Miss H. Sukova
*Miss K. Jordan and Mrs. P. D. Smylie*
1991—Miss L. Savchenko and Miss N. Zvereva
*Miss G. Fernandez and Miss J. Novotna*
1992—Miss G. Fernandez and Miss N. Zvereva
*Miss J. Novotna and Mrs L. Savchenko-Neiland*

## MAIDEN NAMES OF LADY CHAMPIONS

In the above tables the following have been recorded in both married and single identities.

| | | | | | |
|---|---|---|---|---|---|
| *Mrs. R. Cawley* | *Miss E. F. Goolagong* | *Mrs. G. W. Hillyard* | *Miss B. Bingley* | *Mrs. L. E. G. Price* | *Miss S. Reynolds* |
| *Mrs. Lambert Chambers* | *Miss D. K. Douglass* | *Mrs. P. F. Jones* | *Miss A. S. Haydon* | *Miss G. E. Reid* | *Miss K. Melville* |
| *Mrs. B. M. Court* | *Miss M. Smith* | *Mrs. L. W. King* | *Miss B. J. Moffitt* | *Mrs. P. D. Smylie* | *Miss E. M. Sayers* |
| *Mrs. B. C. Covell* | *Miss P. L. Howkins* | *Mrs. M. R. King* | *Miss P. E. Mudford* | *Frau S. Sperling* | *Fraulein H. Krahwinkel* |
| *Mrs. D. E. Dalton* | *Miss J. A. M. Tegart* | *Mrs. D. R. Larcombe* | *Miss E. W. Thomson* | *Mrs. A. Sterry* | *Miss C. Cooper* |
| *Mrs. W. du Pont* | *Miss M. Osborne* | *Mrs. J. M. Lloyd* | *Miss C. M. Evert* | *Mrs. J. R. Susman* | *Miss K. Hantze* |
| *Mrs. L. A. Godfree* | *Miss K. McKane* | *Mrs. F. S. Moody* | *Miss H. Wills* | | |
| *Mrs. H. F. Gourlay Cawley* | *Miss H. F. Gourlay* | *Mrs. O. Morozova* | *Miss O. Morozova* | | |

NOTE.—For the years 1913, 1914 and 1919-1923 inclusive the above records include the "World's Championship on Grass" granted to The Lawn Tennis Association by The International Lawn Tennis Federation. This title was then abolished and commencing in 1924 they became The Official Lawn Tennis Championships recognised by The International Lawn Tennis Federation. Prior to 1922 the holders in the Singles Events and Gentlemen's Doubles did not compete in the Championships but met the winners of these events in the Challenge Rounds.
†Challenge Round abolished: holders subsequently played through. ★The holder did not defend the title.

# THE CHAMPIONSHIP ROLL

## MIXED DOUBLES

1913—Hope Crisp and Mrs. C. O. Tuckey
    *J. C. Parke and Mrs. D. R. Larcombe*
1914—J. C. Parke and Mrs. D. R. Larcombe
    *A. F. Wilding and Mlle. Broquedis*
1919—R. Lycett and Miss E. Ryan
    *A. D. Prebble and Mrs. Lambert Chambers*
1920—G. L. Patterson and Mlle. S. Lenglen
    *R. Lycett and Miss E. Ryan*
1921—R. Lycett and Miss E. Ryan
    *M. Woosnam and Miss P. L. Howkins*
1922—P. O'Hara-Wood and Mlle. S. Lenglen
    *R. Lycett and Miss E. Ryan*
1923—R. Lycett and Miss E. Ryan
    *L. S. Deane and Mrs. D. C. Shepherd-Barron*
1924—J. B. Gilbert and Miss K. McKane
    *L. A. Godfree and Mrs. D. C. Shepherd-Barron*
1925—J. Borotra and Mlle. S. Lenglen
    *H. L. de Morpurgo and Miss E. Ryan*
1926—L. A. Godfree and Mrs. L. A. Godfree
    *H. Kinsey and Miss M. K. Browne*
1927—F. T. Hunter and Miss E. Ryan
    *L. A. Godfree and Mrs. L. A. Godfree*
1928—P. D. B. Spence and Miss E. Ryan
    *J. Crawford and Miss D. Akhurst*
1929—F. T. Hunter and Miss H. Wills
    *I. G. Collins and Miss J. Fry*
1930—J. H. Crawford and Miss E. Ryan
    *D. Prenn and Fraulein H. Krahwinkel*
1931—G. M. Lott and Mrs. L. A. Harper
    *I. G. Collins and Miss J. C. Ridley*
1932—E. Maier and Miss E. Ryan
    *H. C. Hopman and Mlle. J. Sigart*
1933—G. von Cramm and Fraulein H. Krahwinkel
    *N. G. Farquharson and Miss M. Heeley*
1934—R. Miki and Miss D. E. Round
    *H. W. Austin and Mrs. D. C. Shepherd-Barron*
1935—F. J. Perry and Miss D. E. Round
    *H. C. Hopman and Mrs. H. C. Hopman*
1936—F. J. Perry and Miss D. E. Round
    *J. D. Budge and Mrs. S. P. Fabyan*
1937—J. D. Budge and Miss A. Marble
    *Y. Petra and Mme. R. Mathieu*
1938—J. D. Budge and Miss A. Marble
    *H. Henkel and Mrs. S. P. Fabyan*
1939—R. L. Riggs and Miss A. Marble
    *F. H. D. Wilde and Miss N. B. Brown*
1946—T. Brown and Miss L. Brough
    *G. E. Brown and Miss D. Bundy*

1947—J. E. Bromwich and Miss L. Brough
    *C. F. Long and Mrs. N. M. Bolton*
1948—J. E. Bromwich and Miss L. Brough
    *F. A. Sedgman and Miss D. Hart*
1949—E. W. Sturgess and Mrs. S. P. Summers
    *J. E. Bromwich and Miss L. Brough*
1950—E. W. Sturgess and Miss L. Brough
    *G. E. Brown and Mrs. P. C. Todd*
1951—F. A. Sedgman and Miss D. Hart
    *M. G. Rose and Mrs. N. M. Bolton*
1952—F. A. Sedgman and Miss D. Hart
    *E. Morea and Mrs. T. D. Long*
1953—V. Seixas and Miss D. Hart
    *E. Morea and Miss S. Fry*
1954—V. Seixas and Miss D. Hart
    *K. R. Rosewall and Mrs. W. du Pont*
1955—V. Seixas and Miss D. Hart
    *E. Morea and Miss L. Brough*
1956—V. Seixas and Miss S. Fry
    *G. Mulloy and Miss A. Gibson*
1957—M. G. Rose and Miss D. R. Hard
    *N. A. Fraser and Miss A. Gibson*
1958—R. N. Howe and Miss L. Coghlan
    *K. Nielsen and Miss A. Gibson*
1959—R. Laver and Miss D. R. Hard
    *N. A. Fraser and Miss M. E. Bueno*
1960—R. Laver and Miss D. R. Hard
    *R. N. Howe and Miss M. E. Bueno*
1961—F. S. Stolle and Miss L. R. Turner
    *R. N. Howe and Miss E. Buding*
1962—N. A. Fraser and Mrs. W. du Pont
    *R. D. Ralston and Miss A. S. Haydon*
1963—K. N. Fletcher and Miss M. Smith
    *R. A. J. Hewitt and Miss D. R. Hard*
1964—F. S. Stolle and Miss L. R. Turner
    *K. N. Fletcher and Miss M. Smith*
1965—K. N. Fletcher and Miss M. Smith
    *A. D. Roche and Miss J. A. M. Tegart*
1966—K. N. Fletcher and Miss M. Smith
    *R. D. Ralston and Mrs. L. W. King*
1967—O. K. Davidson and Mrs. L. W. King
    *K. N. Fletcher and Miss M. E. Bueno*
1968—K. N. Fletcher and Mrs. B. M. Court
    *A. Metreveli and Miss O. Morozova*
1969—F. S. Stolle and Mrs. P. F. Jones
    *A. D. Roche and Miss J. A. M. Tegart*
1970—I. Nastase and Miss R. Casals
    *A. Metreveli and Miss O. Morozova*

1971—O. K. Davidson and Mrs. L. W. King
    *M. C. Riessen and Mrs. B. M. Court*
1972—I. Nastase and Miss R. Casals
    *K. G. Warwick and Miss E. F. Goolagong*
1973—O. K. Davidson and Mrs. L. W. King
    *R. Ramirez and Miss J. S. Newberry*
1974—O. K. Davidson and Mrs. L. W. King
    *M. J. Farrell and Miss L. J. Charles*
1975—M. C. Riessen and Mrs. B. M. Court
    *A. J. Stone and Miss B. F. Stove*
1976—A. D. Roche and Miss F. Durr
    *R. L. Stockton and Miss R. Casals*
1977—R. A. J. Hewitt and Miss G. R. Stevens
    *F. D. McMillan and Miss B. F. Stove*
1978—F. D. McMillan and Miss B. F. Stove
    *R. O. Ruffels and Mrs. L. W. King*
1979—R. A. J. Hewitt and Miss G. R. Stevens
    *F. D. McMillan and Miss B. F. Stove*
1980—J. R. Austin and Miss T. Austin
    *M. R. Edmondson and Miss D. L. Fromholtz*
1981—F. D. McMillan and Miss B. F. Stove
    *J. R. Austin and Miss T. Austin*
1982—K. Curren and Miss A. E. Smith
    *J. M. Lloyd and Miss W. M. Turnbull*
1983—J. M. Lloyd and Miss W. M. Turnbull
    *S. Denton and Mrs. L. W. King*
1984—J. M. Lloyd and Miss W. M. Turnbull
    *S. Denton and Miss K. Jordan*
1985—P. McNamee and Miss M. Navratilova
    *J. B. Fitzgerald and Mrs. P. D. Smylie*
1986—K. Flach and Miss K. Jordan
    *H. P. Guenthardt and Miss M. Navratilova*
1987—M. J. Bates and Miss J. M. Durie
    *D. Cahill and Miss N. Provis*
1988—S. E. Stewart and Miss Z. L. Garrison
    *K. Jones and Mrs. S. W. Magers*
1989—J. Pugh and Miss J. Novotna
    *M. Kratzmann and Miss J. M. Byrne*
1990—R. Leach and Miss Z. L. Garrison
    *J. B. Fitzgerald and Mrs. P. D. Smylie*
1991—J. B. Fitzgerald and Mrs. P. D. Smylie
    *J. Pugh and Miss N. Zvereva*
1992—C. Suk and Mrs L. Savchenko-Neiland
    *J. Eltingh and Miss M. Oremans*

# THE JUNIORS CHAMPIONSHIP ROLL

## BOYS' SINGLES

1948—S. Stockenberg (Sweden)
1949—S. Stockenberg (Sweden)
1950—J. A. T. Horn (G.B.)
1951—J. Kupferburger (S.A.)
1952—R. K. Wilson (G.B.)
1953—W. A. Knight (G.B.)
1954—R. Krishnan (India)
1955—M. P. Hann (G.B.)
1956—R. Holmberg (U.S.A.)
1957—J. I. Tattersall (G.B.)
1958—E. Buchholz (U.S.A.)
1959—T. Lejus (U.S.S.R.)

1960—A. R. Mandelstam (S.A.)
1961—C. E. Graebner (U.S.A.)
1962—S. Matthews (G.B.)
1963—N. Kalogeropoulos (Greece)
1964—I. El Shafei (U.A.R.)
1965—V. Korotkov (U.S.S.R.)
1966—V. Korotkov (U.S.S.R.)
1967—M. Orantes (Spain)
1968—J. G. Alexander (Australia)
1969—B. Bertram (S.A.)
1970—B. Bertram (S.A.)
1971—R. Kreiss (U.S.A.)

1972—B. Borg (Sweden)
1973—W. Martin (U.S.A.)
1974—W. Martin (U.S.A.)
1975—C. J. Lewis (N.Z.)
1976—H. Guenthardt (Switzerland)
1977—V. A. Winitsky (U.S.A.)
1978—I. Lendl (Czechoslovakia)
1979—R. Krishnan (India)
1980—T. Tulasne (France)
1981—M. W. Anger (U.S.A.)
1982—P. Cash (Australia)
1983—S. Edberg (Sweden)

1984—M. Kratzmann (Australia)
1985—L. Lavalle (Mexico)
1986—E. Velez (Mexico)
1987—D. Nargisco (Italy)
1988—N. Pereira (Venezuela)
1989—N. Kulti (Sweden)
1990—L. Paes (India)
1991—T. Enqvist (Sweden)
1992—D. Skoch (Czechoslovakia)

## BOYS' DOUBLES

1982—P. Cash and J. Frawley
1983—M. Kratzmann and S. Youl
1984—R. Brown and R. Weiss
1985—A. Moreno and J. Yzaga

1986—T. Carbonnell and P. Korda
1987—J. Stoltenberg and T. Woodbridge
1988—J. Stoltenberg and T. Woodbridge
1989—J. Palmer and J. Stark

1990—S. Lareau and S. Leblanc
1991—K. Alami and G. Rusedski
1992—S. Baldas and S. Draper

## GIRLS' SINGLES

1948—Miss O. Miskova (Czechoslovakia)
1949—Miss C. Mercelis (Belgium)
1950—Miss L. Cornell (G.B.)
1951—Miss L. Cornell (G.B.)
1952—Miss ten Bosch (Netherlands)
1953—Miss D. Kilian (S.A.)
1954—Miss V. A. Pitt (G.B.)
1955—Miss S. M. Armstrong (G.B.)
1956—Miss A. S. Haydon (G.B.)
1957—Miss M. Arnold (U.S.A.)
1958—Miss S. M. Moore (U.S.A.)
1959—Miss J. Cross (S.A.)

1960—Miss K. Hantze (U.S.A.)
1961—Miss G. Baksheeva (U.S.S.R.)
1962—Miss G. Baksheeva (U.S.S.R.)
1963—Miss D. M. Salfati (France)
1964—Miss P. Bartkowicz (U.S.A.)
1965—Miss O. Morozova (U.S.S.R.)
1966—Miss B. Lindstrom (Finland)
1967—Miss J. Salome (Netherlands)
1968—Miss K. Pigeon (U.S.A.)
1969—Miss K. Sawamatsu (Japan)
1970—Miss S. Walsh (U.S.A.)
1971—Miss M. Kroschina (U.S.S.R.)

1972—Miss I. Kloss (S.A.)
1973—Miss A. Kiyomura (U.S.A.)
1974—Miss M Jausovec (Yugoslavia)
1975—Miss N. Y. Chmyreva (U.S.S.R.)
1976—Miss N. Y. Chmyreva (U.S.S.R.)
1977—Miss L. Antonoplis (U.S.A.)
1978—Miss T. Austin (U.S.A.)
1979—Miss M. L. Piatek (U.S.A.)
1980—Miss D. Freeman (Australia)
1981—Miss Z. Garrison (U.S.A.)
1982—Miss C. Tanvier (France)
1983—Miss P. Paradis (France)

1984—Miss A. N. Croft (G.B.)
1985—Miss A. Holikova (Czechoslovakia)
1986—Miss N. Zvereva (U.S.S.R.)
1987—Miss N. Zvereva (U.S.S.R.)
1988—Miss B. Schultz (Netherlands)
1989—Miss A. Strnadova (Czechoslovakia)
1990—Miss A. Strnadova (Czechoslovakia)
1991—Miss B. Rittner (Germany)
1992—Miss C. Rubin (U.S.A.)

## GIRLS' DOUBLES

1982—Miss B. Herr and Miss P. Barg
1983—Miss P. Fendick and Miss P. Hy
1984—Miss C. Kuhlman and Miss S. Rehe
1985—Miss L. Field and Miss J. Thompson

1986—Miss M. Jaggard and Miss L. O'Neill
1987—Miss N. Medvedeva and Miss N. Zvereva
1988—Miss J.-A. Faull and Miss R. McQuillan
1989—Miss J. Capriati and Miss M. McGrath

1990—Miss K. Habsudova and Miss A. Strnadova
1991—Miss C. Barclay and Miss L. Zaltz
1992—Miss M. Avotins and Miss L. McShea